Praise for *The Best American Poetry*

"Each year, a vivid snapshot of what a distinguished poet finds exciting, fresh, and memorable: and over the years, as good a comprehensive overview of contemporary poetry as there can be."

—Robert Pinsky

"*The Best American Poetry* series has become one of the mainstays of the poetry publication world. For each volume, a guest editor is enlisted to cull the collective output of large and small literary journals published that year to select seventy-five of the year's 'best' poems. The guest editor is also asked to write an introduction to the collection, and the anthologies would be indispensable for these essays alone; combined with [David] Lehman's 'state-of-poetry' forewords and the guest editors' introductions, these anthologies seem to capture the zeitgeist of the current attitudes in American poetry."

—Academy of American Poets

"A high volume of poetic greatness . . . in all of these volumes . . . there is brilliance, there is innovation, there are surprises."

—*Publishers Weekly* (starred review)

"A year's worth of the very best!"

—*People*

"A preponderance of intelligent, straightforward poems."

—*Booklist*

"A 'best' anthology that really lives up to its title."

—*Chicago Tribune*

"An essential purchase."

—*The Washington Post*

"For the small community of American poets, *The Best American Poetry* is the *Michelin Guide*, the *Reader's Digest*, and the Prix Goncourt."

—*ᵢservateur*

T0182635

THE
BEST
AMERICAN
POETRY
2024

◇　◇　◇

Mary Jo Salter, Editor

David Lehman, Series Editor

SCRIBNER POETRY

NEW YORK　LONDON　TORONTO　SYDNEY　NEW DELHI

Scribner Poetry
An Imprint of Simon & Schuster, LLC
1230 Avenue of the Americas
New York, NY 10020

First Scribner Poetry edition September 2024

SCRIBNER POETRY and design are trademarks of Simon & Schuster, LLC

Simon & Schuster: Celebrating 100 Years of Publishing in 2024

For information about special discounts for bulk purchases, please contact Simon &
Schuster Special Sales at 1-866-506-1949 or business@simonandschuster.com.

The Simon & Schuster Speakers Bureau can bring authors to your live event. For more
information or to book an event, contact the Simon & Schuster Speakers Bureau at
1-866-248-3049 or visit our website at www.simonspeakers.com.

Manufactured in the United States of America

1   3   5   7   9   10   8   6   4   2

Library of Congress Control Number: 88644281

ISBN 978-1-9821-8680-7
ISBN 978-1-9821-8679-1 (pbk)
ISBN 978-1-9821-8681-4 (ebook)

CONTENTS

Foreword by David Lehman — xi

Introduction by Mary Jo Salter — xxiii

Kim Addonizio, "Existential Elegy" — 1

Howard Altmann, "Kyiv" — 3

Julia Alvarez, "Amenorrhea" — 4

Catherine Barnett, "Apophasis at the All-Night Rite Aid" — 5

Joshua Bennett, "First Philosophy" — 6

April Bernard, "'Sithens in a net'" — 8

Christopher Childers, "Miasma" — 10

Ama Codjoe, "The Deer" — 11

Henri Cole, "At Sixty-Five" — 12

Billy Collins, "The Monet Conundrum" — 14

Brendan Constantine, "Cleptopolitan" — 15

Armen Davoudian, "Conscription" — 17

Kwame Dawes, "The Remnant" — 18

Timothy Donnelly, "The Bard of Armagh" — 19

Rita Dove, "Happy End" — 21

Joanne Dominique Dwyer, "Irish Traveler's Writer's Block" — 23

Elaine Equi, "Avoidance" — 25

Gabriella Fee, "A Lighthouse Keeper Considers Love" — 27

Brandel France de Bravo, "After the Ecstasy, the Laundry" — 29

Dana Gioia, "Satan's Management Style" — 31

Louise Glück, "Passion and Form" — 33

Amy Glynn, "Space Is the Final Frontier" — 34

Jessica Greenbaum, "Each Other Moment" — 37

Rachel Hadas, "Voyage" — 39

Saskia Hamilton, "All Souls" — 40

Jeffrey Harrison, "A Message from Tony Hoagland" — 42

Terrance Hayes, "How to Fold" — 44

John Hennessy, "Domestic Retrograde" — 46

W. J. Herbert, "Pando's Grove" — 48

Richie Hofmann, "Lamb" — 49

Marie Howe, "Chainsaw" — 51

Omotara James, "Closure" — 52

Eve Jones, "Japan" — 54

George Kalogeris, "Byzantine Chanting" — 55

Stephen Kampa, "Someone Else's Gift" — 57

Richard Kenney, "Self's the Man" — 58

Karl Kirchwey, "*Kiss Me Deadly* (1955)" — 59

Yusef Komunyakaa, "My Brothers, the Olmec" — 60

David Lehman, from *Ithaca* — 62

Ada Limón, "In Praise of Mystery: A Poem for Europa" — 68

Sarah Luczaj, "Shopping Lists" — 69

Amit Majmudar, "Charmed Life" — 71

Clarence Major, "Weather Conditions" — 72

Charles Martin, "You Summon Me . . ." — 73

Heather McHugh, "Two Widows, Making a Bed" — 80

Maggie Millner, from *Couplets* — 82

Ange Mlinko, "The Open C" — 87

Andrew Motion, "The Explanation" — 88

Paul Muldoon, "Joy in Service on Rue Tagore" — 90

Harryette Mullen, "Haiku Garden" — 92

Jesse Nathan, "Dame's Rocket" — 93

Jacqueline Osherow, "Fast Track: Beijing, Montana, Harlem" — 94

Rowan Ricardo Phillips, "The First and Final Poem Is the Sun" — 99

Robert Pinsky, "Proverbs of Limbo" — 100

Maya C. Popa, "What's Unsaid" — 102

Vidyan Ravinthiran, "Eelam" — 103

Natalie Scenters-Zapico, "Sentimental Evening" — 104

Robyn Schiff, from *Information Desk: An Epic* — 106

Gjertrud Schnackenberg, "Strike Into It Unasked" — 108

Grace Schulman, "Night Visitor" — 116

Jane Shore, "The Hat" — 117

Mitch Sisskind, "Jack Benny" — 121

Maggie Smith, "Hope Chest" — 122

Karen Solie, "The Bluebird" — 123

Christopher Spaide, "I'm Not Dying, You're Dying" — 125

A. E. Stallings, "Crown Shyness" — 127

Mark Strand, "Wallace Stevens Comes Back to Read His Poems at the 92nd Street Y" — 131

Adrienne Su, "The Days" — 133

Arthur Sze, "Pe'ahi Light" — 135

Claire Wahmanholm, "The Field Is Hot and Hotter" — 139

Rosanna Warren, "A New Year" — 140

Michael Waters, "Ashkenazi Birthmark" — 141

Eliot Weinberger, from *The Life of Tu Fu* — 142

Matthew Yeager, "The Man with the Yellow Balloon" — 146

Kevin Young, "Diptych" — 153

Contributors' Notes and Comments — 157

Magazines Where the Poems Were First Published — 197

Acknowledgments — 201

DAVID LEHMAN was born in New York City in 1948, the son of Holocaust survivors. A graduate of Stuyvesant High School and Columbia University, he spent two years at Clare College, Cambridge, as a Kellett Fellow. Upon his return to New York, he worked as Lionel Trilling's research assistant and earned his PhD at Columbia with a thesis on prose poems. He taught for four years at Hamilton College, and then, after a postdoctoral fellowship at Cornell, he turned to writing as a full-time occupation. Lehman launched *The Best American Poetry* series in 1988. He edited *The Oxford Book of American Poetry* (2006). *The Morning Line* (University of Pittsburgh Press, 2021) is the most recent of his poetry collections; his prose books include *The Mysterious Romance of Murder* (Cornell University Press, 2022), *One Hundred Autobiographies: A Memoir* (Cornell, 2019), and *Signs of the Times: Deconstruction and the Fall of Paul de Man* (Simon & Schuster, 1991). In 2010 he received the Deems Taylor Award from the American Society of Composers, Authors, and Publishers (ASCAP) for *A Fine Romance: Jewish Songwriters, American Songs* (Schocken, 2009). Lehman lives in New York City and in Ithaca, New York.

FOREWORD

by David Lehman

◊   ◊   ◊

Lord Byron had a knack for the clever stanza-closing couplet in *Don Juan*, his comic masterwork, but his lines on John Keats's death miss the mark. "'Tis strange, the mind, that very fiery particle, / Should let itself be snuffed out by an article," Byron wrote. The *Quarterly Review* did trash Keats's efforts. But he died young—shy of his twenty-sixth birthday—not from insult but from an acute case of consumption. He knew he was dying. "An English winter would put an end to me, and do so in a lingering hateful manner," Keats wrote in a letter to the slightly older Percy Bysshe Shelley. "Therefore, I must either voyage or journey to Italy, as a soldier marches up to a battery." In Italy he died.

Asked to name the first poem that profoundly moved them, some readers opt for Keats's "When I Have Fears," which he wrote in January 1818, just three years before his death from tuberculosis. Even if you didn't know that Keats died at age twenty-five, this immortal sonnet is bound to affect you. No other poem treats the fear of death, and in particular an untimely death, in so noble a fashion:

> When I have fears that I may cease to be
> Before my pen has glean'd my teeming brain,
> Before high-piled books, in charact'ry,
> Hold like rich garners the full-ripen'd grain;
> When I behold, upon the night's starr'd face,
> Huge cloudy symbols of a high romance,
> And think that I may never live to trace
> Their shadows, with the magic hand of chance;
> And when I feel, fair creature of an hour!

That I shall never look upon thee more,
Never have relish in the faery power
Of unreflecting love!—then on the shore
Of the wide world I stand alone, and think
Till Love and Fame to nothingness do sink.

Adhering to the structure of a Shakespearean sonnet, the poem consists of just one sentence stretched over fourteen lines. The first twelve advance the theme in three four-line movements (beginning "When," "When," and "And when"). The eloquent closing couplet provides the "then" on which all these dependent clauses rest. It raises the poem from trepidation to a kind of visionary heroism.

Keats wastes no time. He opens with startling directness, ten monosyllables in a row: "When I have fears that I may cease to be." Then he turns to metaphor: "Before my pen has glean'd my teeming brain." Keats uses the verb "to glean" in its original sense of "to gather for a harvest." The "pen" and "brain" specify that it is a writer who is contemplating his demise, but "glean'd" does double duty, likening the act of writing to that of bringing forth the fruit of the earth.

A rich simile concludes the first movement of the poem: "Before high-piled books, in charact'ry, / Hold like rich garners the full-ripen'd grain." Keats uses "in charact'ry" as we would say "in print"; he is imagining the grandeur of publication. Note the double alliteration—"rich garners," "ripen'd grain"—that makes the line so characteristic of a poet whose words you can almost taste. Or would, if you possessed the "strenuous tongue" that "can burst Joy's grape against his palate fine," to quote from Keats's "Ode on Melancholy."

The sonnet's second movement changes the metaphorical terrain from earth to sky, from writing to seeing, and from books to stars: "When I behold, upon the night's starr'd face, / Huge cloudy symbols of a high romance." The very word "romance" signals the theme of the poem's third movement. From stellar glory we move to "unreflecting love," the love of a "fair creature of an hour," a love doomed to go unfulfilled, unrequited.

In his masterly study *Shakespeare*, the scholar and poet Mark Van

Doren argued that the weak part of a Shakespeare sonnet may be its closing couplet.[1] Not here. "Then on the shore / Of the wide world I stand alone, and think / Till Love and Fame to nothingness do sink." As he positions himself at the edge of the world, in intense contemplation of a dire fate, Keats arrives at a transcendent moment. He transports himself into an almost palpable "nothingness" that makes all hope of "love and fame" seem somehow vain and irrelevant. It is as if the poet can feel, can "think" his way into feeling, the annihilation of consciousness—as if he can apprehend the oblivion that he intends to meet head-on. The subtle pauses between these lines enhance their impact. The couplet exists in counterpoint to this amazing sentence from the last of his deathbed letters: "I have an habitual feeling of my real life having past, and that I am leading a posthumous existence."

In another of his poignant and profound letters, Keats develops his concept of "negative capability," a phrase that has launched a thousand fellowships. Keats explains that "the excellence of every art is its intensity, capable of making all disagreeables evaporate." The observation can help to illuminate the logic of his otherwise hard-to-grasp assertion that "Beauty is truth, truth beauty." *King Lear* is Keats's example of how greatness of poetry can transform ugly truth into artistic beauty.

"When I Have Fears" is a second example of Keats's negative capability in practice. Keats describes his fears in a heartbreaking way. But it is as if he can produce verbally what he will not be able to experience. His intensity, his acceptance of what fate has in store, and his fearless resolution substantiate Lionel Trilling's belief that Keats exemplified nothing less than "the poet as hero."

★ ★ ★

Some things don't change. It seems someone is always announcing the death of poetry with nearly the same breathless urgency of Nietzsche

---

1. "Only the 71st [sonnet] maintains its music to the ending syllable. The others die as poetry at the couplet, or cease somewhat less suddenly at the close of a quatrain." *Shakespeare* (New York Review Books Classics, 2005), p. 4.

asserting the demise of God. "Poetry Died 100 Years Ago This Month" ran the headline of a piece in *The New York Times* on December 29, 2022. Matthew Walther, the author, goes over previous "autopsy reports," before trotting out his own theory, which is that T. S. Eliot "finished poetry off" in *The Waste Land* (1922). "The problem," Walther contends, "is not that Eliot put poetry on the wrong track. It's that he went as far down that track as anyone could, exhausting its possibilities and leaving little or no work for those who came after him." The statement leaves unclear whether the "track" Eliot went down was either the wrong one or possibly a poetics equal to the disjunctions of modern life. In any case, as Walther sees it, poetry has disappeared, except perhaps for MFA programs, which he calls "a luxe version of life support."

Poetry claimed its honorable place in one of the year's most celebrated films, Christopher Nolan's *Oppenheimer*. The physicist who supervised the building of the atom bomb came up with "Trinity" as a code name for the first test in July 1945. Why? Because of John Donne's "Holy Sonnet #14," which the movie quotes. The poem begins "Batter my heart, three-person'd God." Full of paradox in Donne's best manner—"Take me to you, imprison me, for I, / Except you enthrall me, never shall be free"—the sonnet is quite apt for the intense contradictory impulses in J. Robert Oppenheimer's mind.

To poetry I turn for relief from the ferocity of hatred that has come more and more to define our public discourse. Poetry, especially great poetry, is my favored mode of resistance in the teeth of bestial violence, rabid tribalism, false accusations, and the shaming that is our digital equivalent of the ritual stoning undergone by Tessie Hutchinson, the unlucky woman who draws the slip marked with the black spot in Shirley Jackson's story "The Lottery."

Only in the dialogue between reader and writer can poetry defeat its enemies: rage, terror, dread, prejudice, cruelty, greed, violence. No poem will end a war, or protect the innocent who are its casualties, but all art worthy of the name stands up for life, love, the act of creation, the liberty of the mind, the vital realm of the imagination. Poetry, in Wallace Stevens's words, presses back against "the pressure of reality." Stevens argues that "individuals of extraordinary imagination" can "cancel" the pressure by resisting it. Like all stays against confusion, it is momentary in its consolation though immortal as a source of inspiration.

★ ★ ★

Nobel laureate Louise Glück, wonderful poet and friend, died at the age of eighty on Friday the 13th of October 2023. Louise edited *The Best American Poetry 1993*, and the experience of working closely with her—primarily by old-fashioned mail and the occasional phone call—was unforgettable. She took on the job despite a natural inclination to remain "on the sidelines, preferably the very front of the sidelines." In a moment of moral clarity characteristic of Louise, she recognized that "continuous refusal to expose my judgment to public scrutiny seemed vanity and self-protection." When the year began, Louise clamored for literary magazines "like a person in a restaurant banging the table for service," in her words. They came, so many you could fill a small office with them.

Louise proved herself to be a peerless close reader of poems, and when I said this to her, she, usually distrustful of compliments, seemed genuinely touched. She chose the contents of the volume with "the generosity on which exacting criticism depends." And she paid me the compliment of treating me like a partner in the enterprise; her decisions were final, but she welcomed discussion, and it was fun exchanging views.

In a biographical note written for the Nobel Prize committee, Louise wrote that growing up she was good at school, not so good at "the social world," and that during adolescence she felt "ostracized" everywhere but summer camp. As a student at Columbia, she came under the influence of Stanley Kunitz, who championed her work. His "endorsement of high ambition" continued to inspire her, though "there was a deep fissure" with her erstwhile mentor when she strove to banish figurative language from the poems in her 1990 book, *Ararat*. It signaled a new direction for her, and it was precisely the poems in *Ararat* and in the volume that succeeded it, *The Wild Iris*, that made me feel that Louise was writing the best poems of her life and we would be lucky if she agreed to take the helm of the 1993 edition of *The Best American Poetry*. In a moving remembrance in *The Paris Review*, Elisa Gonzalez wrote, "I trace what feels like her love for me. She read. She listened. She critiqued. She encouraged. She nagged. Her faith in me exceeded my faith in myself."

In this year's *Best American Poetry*, we have a three-line poem by Louise Glück, "Passion and Form," in addition to work by other poets who have served as guest editors in this series as long ago as 1991 and as recently as 2023: in chronological order, Mark Strand, Rita Dove, Yusef Komunyakaa, Paul Muldoon, Billy Collins, Heather McHugh, Kevin Young, Terrance Hayes, Dana Gioia, and Elaine Equi. We have poems that embrace the fruitful exigencies of rhyme and form: the sonnet sequence, the Rubáiyát stanza, couplets, haiku stanzas, free verse that lends itself to two-line or three-line stanzas, a meditation on the poetry of Gerard Manley Hopkins. There are arresting titles: "Satan's Management Style," "Wallace Stevens Comes Back to Read His Poems at the 92nd Street Y." I regret that I could not prevail upon Mary Jo Salter, our guest editor, to choose "The Mailman," a poem of hers that exemplifies the virtues that made me feel she would be an excellent editor for the *BAP* series.

Mary Jo has abundant editorial experience. After graduating from Harvard, where she studied with Elizabeth Bishop, she read for *The Atlantic* and was one of the first to recognize Amy Clampitt's brilliance. As poetry editor at *The New Republic*, she got used to having sacks of submissions deposited on her doorstep. As an editor of the hugely influential *Norton Anthology of Poetry*, she understands the demands and complexities of putting together an ambitious anthology. She writes beautifully on the poets she loves. In an essay on W. H. Auden published last year in *Literary Matters*, she reveals the secret of the last line in his "Epitaph on a Tyrant": "And when he cried the little children died in the streets."[2]

It is as a poet that Mary Jo Salter has distinguished herself among her contemporaries. She uses the conventions and devices of poetry to confront, with rare humility, the radical changes and problems we

---

2. See what happens when you switch the verbs in the line.

face in the twenty-first century. A humane and compassionate intelligence informs her work. She writes with subtlety, self-awareness, and an utter delight in wordplay. Errors of speech can function as implicit metaphors, as in "Last Words," which appeared on the *BAP* blog on January 20, 2023:

Forgive me for not writing sober,
I mean sooner, but I almost don't
dare see what I write, I keep mating mistakes,
I mean making, and I'm wandering
if I've inherited what
my father's got.

I first understood it when he tried
to introduce me to somebunny:
"This is my doctor," he said,
then didn't say more, "my daughter."
The man kindly nodded
out the door.
I thought: is this dimension
what I'm headed for?

I mean dementia.
Not Autheimer's, but that kind he has,
possessive aphasia: oh that's good,
I meant to say progressive.
Talk about euthanasia!
I mean euphemasia,
nice words inside your head not there,
and it's not progress at all.

No, he's up against the boil
after years now of a sad, slow wall
and he's so hungry,
I mean angry.

Me too. I need to get my rhymes in
while I still mean. I mean can.[3]

It is rare that metaphysical wit can support a thesis about a poet's fear of aphasia as emblematic of the larger fear of dementia that strikes us even as we live longer lives.

★ ★ ★

In 1988, when this series began, the Internet did not exist. The Berlin Wall had not yet come down. The words of the day were *glasnost*, *perestroika*, and "leveraged buyout." No one had heard of the dot.com bubble, the iPhone, the selfie, the cloud, or Taylor Swift. Some people, not many, had heard of the maverick American inventor, Nikola Tesla. *Time* and *Newsweek* were still important, but the press was more interested in Donna Rice and *Monkey Business* than in Gary Hart's foreign policy ideas, and evidence of plagiarism wiped out Joe Biden's campaign for the presidency. Michael Jordan scored thirty-five points a game and was the NBA's best scorer *and* best defender. Candice Bergen played Murphy Brown, a single mother, on television, and Kirk Gibson hit a home run more improbable than any imagined by Bernard Malamud or the creators of the 1955 musical *Damn Yankees*. Though the crash of October 1987 was still on people's minds, money remained the caffeine of the ambitious. Oliver Stone's *Wall Street* opened with the Twin Towers rising majestically while Frank Sinatra sang "Fly Me to the Moon."

While it remains for others to decide whether the poetry we publish today measures up to that which we perpetuated in our first years, we have done our best to represent the paths poets take when they face a fork, "the many paths / Where triumph rang its brassy phrase, or love / Whispered a little out of tenderness" (Wallace Stevens, "Sunday Morning"). This is the thirty-seventh volume in the series, and if a young academic looking for a thesis subject loves poetry, one could do worse than considering a shelf of *The Best American Poetry* from its origin to the present. We have proved that a book of poetry can matter in the life of a young poet; that poetry can pay for itself, that its publication need

---

3. From *Zoom Rooms* by Mary Jo Salter (Knopf, 2022).

not depend on subsidies or grants; that a concerted effort to single out the best poems of the year can result in an annual rite of autumn; and that our leading poets have, with generosity and acumen, surveyed the scene and left a record of their predilections.

In May 2008, the students in my graduate seminar, accustomed as they were to writing poems based on my prompts, came up with a prompt of their own. As we approached the end of the semester, they asked me to deliver a valedictory address. I gave them John Donne's poem "A Valediction: Forbidding Mourning," in which a lover assures his beloved that his goodbye is temporary. To indicate that the speaker has a round-trip, not a one-way ticket, Donne uses the audacious conceit of a mathematical compass, the legs of which describe a circle—an image of perfection, suitable for a union of equals after a brief separation.

The students liked Donne all right, and they agreed to read the metaphysical poets during the summer, but they wanted a real farewell address—advice on being a poet in an era that militates against poetry.

This is what I said:

- Your poems don't have to change the world. They just have to give pleasure. Don't feel you need to make sense all the time. Nor should you shy away from sentiment and feeling.

- You can do anything. When planning your future, do not limit yourself to conventional career paths and to academic jobs dependent on advanced degrees. Do not take out a loan to sustain your poetry habit. You can combine anything with poetry; you can be a poet and also a librarian, an advertising copywriter, a corporate executive, a lawyer, a doctor, an actor, a computer geek, a real estate agent, a soldier, an arts administrator, a journalist.

- Keep trying new things in your poetry. If you can, write every day, even if it is only a few sentences in a notebook. Collaborate with friends. If you're in a fallow period, accept it; sometimes the brain needs time to absorb new experiences. You can always assign yourself a prompt that has worked for you (like a translation from a language you don't understand, or an abecedarius, or a poem by Emily Dickinson as rewritten by Robert Frost). Sometimes a simple reversal of course is all you need to do; if you've been writing present-tense, first-person point-of-view poems, see what happens when you adopt a third-person POV and the past tense.

- Be generous. This may require some effort at diplomacy. But rivalry is not incompatible with friendship. Let posterity decide whose work will endure. We won't be around anyway. Remember that another person's success does nothing to diminish your own achievement. Don't get hung up on prizes. They're great to get; the prestige is nice, the money is nice; but you should spend your time on your writing, your reading, and not on angling to get a lucrative grant. There will come a time when someone else will win the award you deserved, or the job you coveted, or the publication you were banking on. It might even be the person sitting next to you right now. And you will feel envy, you will feel resentment—you wouldn't be human if you didn't. But you cannot afford to give in to these feelings, because envy and resentment, if allowed to fester, can turn easily into bitterness and even spite, and these things are poison to a writer. To ward them off, you will need to go deeper into yourself, into your heart, into the sources of your poetry.
- Avoid politics. Political content tends to create bad poems while accomplishing nothing in the political realm. Slogans reign in politics, and nothing ages so fast as a slogan. Goethe: "the politician will consume the poet."
- Figure out what you need from the world in order to continue as a poet. Sometimes all you need is one magazine editor who believes in your work.
- When you read your poems aloud, do so with conviction. Read slowly and clearly. Read one poem fewer than the time allows. Rehearse so you don't stumble over your own words, the mark of an amateur or an academic.

- Pay no attention to hostile reviewers. Many of them are bullies who think that delivering pain is a mark of authenticity. And when it is your turn to write about others, resist the impulse to give pain—it's not good for your soul. And you do have a soul. Otherwise, you would never have committed your life to poetry.

MARY JO SALTER was born in 1954 in Grand Rapids, Michigan, and grew up there, in Detroit, and in Baltimore. After graduation from Harvard, she took a two-year degree in English at New Hall (now Murray Edwards College), Cambridge. She was a staff editor at *The Atlantic* before moving to Kyoto, Japan, where she taught English for three years. Western Massachusetts, where she was Emily Dickinson Senior Lecturer at Mount Holyoke College, was her home for two decades. She is now Professor Emerita in The Writing Seminars at Johns Hopkins University, where she taught from 2007 to 2022. Former poetry editor of *The New Republic*, coeditor of three editions of *The Norton Anthology of Poetry* (1996, 2005, and 2018), and editor of Amy Clampitt's selected and collected poems, Salter is also an essayist, a lyricist, and a children's book author. She is a member of the American Academy of Arts and Sciences. Her nine collections of poetry, all published by Knopf, include most recently *The Surveyors* (2017) and *Zoom Rooms* (2022). She lives in Baltimore.

INTRODUCTION

by Mary Jo Salter

◇　◇　◇

"I'm Nobody! Who are you?" asked Emily Dickinson. It's clear to many of us who she was and is—one of the greatest poets ever—and certain poems of hers suggest she knew it herself. Still, she had a sense of humor about swelled heads, and we love the zinger that concludes her eight-line Nobody poem:

> How dreary – to be – Somebody!
> How public – like a Frog –
> To tell one's name – the livelong June –
> To an admiring Bog!

Readers delight in these lines because we recognize the empty pomposity that too often afflicts people (that is, *other* people). We also suspect that the hermetic Dickinson (who eschewed publication, dismissing it as "the Auction / Of the Mind of Man") seems specifically to be skewering that subset of people called writers: the people who may have little to tell us other than their bylines, but who look to the admiring "bog" to confirm their brilliance. And among the general class of writers, which includes bestselling novelists and blockbuster screenwriters, we poets risk being the most deluded about our prospect of fame in that bog, now or ever.

Welcome to *The Best American Poetry 2024*, in which (ever since David Lehman inaugurated this annual series in 1988), seventy-five poets, some long established, some newcomers, are rightly saluted publicly for having successfully minded their own business, which is not fame. Or that's what I think, and I'm the person who had the honor to be chosen as guest editor this year. The business of poets, I would argue, includes at least some of these aspirations: to witness the world, including the layered, shifting moods of their own minds' interiors; to feel deeply and also to think through their feelings; to experience life with all of the senses, which sometimes get profitably jumbled; to express some aspect of the human comedy and the human tragedy by exploiting the unique resources of a particular language or languages; to suggest with figures like simile or metaphor the surprising congruity of seemingly unlike things; to speak to their contemporaries about contemporary matters; to place themselves also within the history of humankind, including the history of literature, and to add something to it; to channel our universal musical instincts, our childlike but never merely childish love of song; to dare to remain uncertain and paradoxical and inconclusive as life itself, while also making a finished "thing," a poem, of beauty. The greatest poems may even, in exemplifying beauty, just marginally redefine it, sometimes without the awareness of the reader.

★ ★ ★

2023, the year I was peaceably reading in my chair many hundreds of recent poems that might or might not go into this volume, was a year like many others, in that various forms of violence were rampant worldwide. Some of the poems in this anthology, like its predecessors, find original ways to address past and present violence: a case in point is Michael Waters's "Ashkenazi Birthmark," which I mention for its excellence but also because the magazine in which it first appeared, the admirable *Gettysburg Review*, drew its last breath. So did *Freeman's*, whose final issue contained a brave poem about menopause by Julia Alvarez, "Amenorrhea," in which she writes: "This woman's barrenness / revives the poet's fear— / the line stops here." Alvarez's simple phrase "the line" means three things: our human descendants; the line breaks that add rhythm and suspense to poems; and the future of poetry itself. And if "the line stops"? Hard to say more poetically what we poets fear.

    2023 was also, quietly but not without profound psychic violence, the year that the promises and dangers of artificial intelligence became unignorable in every news source and, indeed, in daily life. Although the term "artificial intelligence" was invented in the 1950s, and its possible applications, ranging from lifesaving surgery to life-obliterating nuclear war, have been in development for a very long time, 2023 was a pivotal year in what I'll call artificial writing. This past year was the one in which the debate about whether students should use ChatGPT in writing their term papers, even their personal essays, became widely acknowledged as moot. Students were doing it, the future was now, and educators could only play catch-up. Some were deeply upset, others shrugged, others felt inspired to harness the technology, to develop whatever good might arise from a fait accompli. And of course it wasn't only educators who felt challenged: so did the writers in Hollywood, who went on strike for five months, and achieved no ban on machines purloining their work, but did win at least some acknowledgment of human authorship after it has been hijacked.

No matter how you or I feel about it, the truth is that a relatively small number of researchers and their investors, working within countries with different kinds of governments and cultures, different notions of what's good for humanity, have stealthily, massively altered the world for all of us; and that includes the world of art. As always happens with "new" technologies, the public is the last to get the memo that major changes are already irreversible. Some of this playing catch-up is happening in the world of poetry. Go to sashastiles.com and you can see what some extremely intelligent people have been doing while you weren't looking: cowriting their poems with machine models. Honorably, these poets acknowledge their collaborations with machines—showing a moral sense that machines themselves, so far, have lacked. Sasha Stiles's book of collaborative poems is the cleverly titled and often clever *Technelegy*. The word itself may make you feel, as I do, behind the curve. Writing this essay in December 2023, I am fairly certain that by Fall 2024, when this book is published, I will have missed mentioning some crucial development.

Yet the most interesting and urgent question to consider is likely to remain Emily Dickinson's: "I'm Nobody! Who are you?" Not long ago, we could laugh at the assertion that each of us is nobody, because it was only partly true. We weren't necessarily important to the world, but we knew that a few family members and friends found us a precious somebody in their own lives, and that collectively, importantly, we were human. We did know that humans change throughout history—that Emily Dickinson's telephone-less family members were at bottom different creatures than a contemporary family with four cell phones at the dinner table. We did know that humans think, feel, and behave differently according to geography and culture, around the world. Still, most of us believed the immutable answer to the question "Who are you?" was that we were human. There was something constant called the human, which, fallible as it is, was not fungible.

Artificial intelligence is already an exponentially greater human-changer even than the Internet—as we keep being told, sometimes in text not written by humans. It's hard for most of us to think beyond the Internet's wholesale changes, but my scariest sci-fi vision of the poetry future goes like this: an ever-growing mass of poetry, both good and bad, is uploaded into machines. Today, the poems that machines write from that data are usually considered bad by humans. But in the near future some machines will begin to write better and better poetry, or at least poetry that humans like (and what's the difference?). Poems written as collaborations between machines and humans will be increasingly liked by humans.

And here's the thing: eventually and indeed quite soon, it won't only be poems that have changed, *human readers will have changed*. We will have been trained by machines to like machine-poems. The percentage of poems written by humans-without-assistance will drop. Over time, new generations of readers will *prefer* machine-written poems to the "canon" of great poetry down the centuries. Do we like the concept of a canon or not? How quaint of us to ask; future readers may no longer be aware of those long centuries' productions. Machine-poems will speak more to us, because (so my fantasy goes) we will be machine-people. Or just machines.

I sometimes wonder whether the current tendency to identify ourselves by nationality, race, religion, ethnicity, gender, sexuality, etc., is at least in part an unconscious reaction to a far greater problem than the oppression of marginalized groups, real and appalling as such oppression is. What we're facing, I think, is the choice by some humans to embrace machine-supremacy.

★ ★ ★

One of the first poems I chose for this volume (and my thanks to David Lehman, who found it in *Alaska Quarterly Review*; indeed, he spotted many other standout poems before I did) was Jessica Greenbaum's "Each Other Moment." The poet densely packs her narrative with the sort of tech-lexicon I've just been discussing, and I'm all for humans doing that. "We were scanning the QR code / to order the iced matcha latte," Greenbaum writes, and incorporates gleefully all the globalized mishmash we talk in—matcha is Japanese, latte is Italian. Cumulatively, artistically, familiar terms take on new meaning: when at the end of the poem "We turned location / back off," Greenbaum isn't just talking about GPS. Similarly, Sarah Luczaj, in a poem called "Shopping Lists" (*AGNI*), uses Google Translate to help her figure out what to send to a friend (nappies? burn gel?) in war-ravaged Ukraine. Or maybe she should just bring the gifts in person? ("Google Maps makes taking the trip / seem a perfectly sane / and logical thing to do. / It would take me 13 hours and 21 minutes.")

Meanwhile, the Covid pandemic may be over, but I couldn't resist featuring a lively poem about its tedium. In a lugubrious poem called "Dockery and Son," Philip Larkin wrote memorably that "Life is first boredom, then fear." True enough, but in the present volume Christopher Childers's XL villanelle from *Smartish Pace*, "Miasma," made me reflect that a global virus flipped the sequence: life is first fear, then boredom. These are the kinds of thoughts poets had in 2023, and it would be a mistake to keep the best of these poems out of anthologies on the argument that they're time-bound. All eras are time-bound: that's what has made them universal.

★ ★ ★

I've been an editor and anthologist, loosely defined, a long time. In a "commonplace book," although I didn't know the term yet, I started copying out my favorite poems at age eleven. (My mother tended to put books of poems in front of me.) One of the first poems recorded in my little notebook, W. B. Yeats's "After Long Silence," concludes: "Bodily decrepitude is wisdom; young / We loved each other and were ignorant." No chance that I knew what decrepitude meant; I must have liked the sound of it, and probably the oddness of that locution "young / We loved each other." Poems usually win us first by means of sound, not meaning. Later I would understand that ending a poem on the word "ignorant" rather than the upbeat "We loved each other" was a very modern thing to do. In large, awkward cursive I also copied out "The Span of Life," a poem of a single couplet, by Robert Frost:

> The old dog barks backward without getting up.
> I can remember when he was a pup.

Well, now I'm the old dog. Except that I like to think I will get up. I don't want to nap my way through my last chapters of life: I want poetry, among other stimulants, to keep me fresh. If you're reading this book, so do you. You may be a poet yourself. Or are you, dear reader, among the many who say that they don't know much about poetry, but they know what they like?

Perfectly reasonable. I can't say why a beautiful poem in your eyes is not a beautiful one in mine, or vice versa. Even after having taken on the daunting responsibility, with several much-revered coeditors, of selecting poems for three different editions (dated 1996, 2005, and 2018) of the 2,000-page, epoch-spanning *Norton Anthology of Poetry*, I still find it almost impossible to come up with Universally Useful Criteria for evaluating a poem. I was once chatting with colleagues on the Writing Seminars faculty at Johns Hopkins about our upcoming deadlines for posting the titles of new literature courses. We teased each other about the trendy titles and overtheorized reading lists we had come up with, and then one of us threw up his hands and said, "Why can't I just call the course Stuff I Like?"

It was an amusing question, but not as naïve as it sounded. Literary anthologies, like literature courses, have always consisted, when you get right down to it, of nothing more or less than stuff that some mortal people liked. True, an editor of a large, comprehensive poetry anthology would be foolhardy and arrogant, if she happens not to like Shakespeare, to attempt erasing the fact of Shakespeare. Still, even Shakespeare started out as stuff liked by his local contemporaries—most of them not poets or playwrights themselves.

Even before embarking on editing this year's *Best American Poetry* I had had the pleasure of reading most of the previous volumes; and I've had my taste broadened, time and again, by guest poet-editors of the past. In the final poem in this book, a former guest editor, Kevin Young, finds himself gazing at paintings in a museum and marvels at "what the world / couldn't say till someone / saw it first": that's what I hope to discover in anthologies too. The editors in this best-poetry series have always done the work of reading plenty of stuff they didn't like in order to arrive at the stuff they liked, distinctive stuff that often sounded nothing like their own poems. A knee-jerk pessimist eager to be course corrected, I find myself this year cheered by the industrious hopefulness, not to mention the stratospheric number, of poets out there. What emerged this year, as in all the *Best American Poetry* volumes, is the work of highly intelligent, feeling, talented people who deserve to be better known. Who merit our attention in this short, precious period we get to be alive.

★ ★ ★

Poets may not be as celebrated as they deserve, but those of us who read them have our favorites whose next appearances we look forward to eagerly. It has always felt like Christmas to me when Gjertrud Schnackenberg, for instance, has new work to show: you'll find in these pages her long, gorgeous poem, "Strike Into It Unasked," about Gerard Manley Hopkins and, more generally, the physical act of writing. It felt like a holiday too to find new poems by the always accomplished Richard Kenney, Paul Muldoon, Jane Shore, Rita Dove, Jeffrey Harrison, Arthur Sze, Rachel Hadas, Kim Addonizio, and more: you'll find here an elegant sample by each. Andrew Motion, former Poet Laureate of the United Kingdom, became an American citizen (that is, a dual citizen) in 2023, and it's a pleasure to represent him in this book with a poem that is haunted by an English childhood. It strikes me that the poets I've mentioned so far, all from my own Boomer generation, demonstrate even in their most emotionally charged poems a more than usual supply of wit. Fortunately, there's plenty of evidence that ingenuity will not die with them: as one example, A. E. Stallings, born 1968, who in 2023 became only the second female in history to be elected Oxford Professor of Poetry, published so many witty-but-serious poems that it was hard to choose among them. I opted for "Crown Shyness," a simply perfect crown of sonnets in *The Sewanee Review*. Younger poets I've followed for a while, such as Christopher Spaide, Ama Codjoe, Armen Davoudian, Maya C. Popa, and Claire Wahmanholm, make their first appearance in this series, as well as poets younger and older whose work I didn't know before, such as Brandel France de Bravo and Omotara James.

An unwritten rule of this series, one which I applaud, is that the guest editor should try to represent as many journals as possible. You won't be surprised, of course, to see multiple poems here from *The New Yorker* or *The New York Review of Books*. I'd like to give a special shout, though, to the editors of smaller magazines—such as Michael Dumanis at *Bennington Review* and John Hennessy at *The Common*— where I always had the nice problem of too many good poems to choose from. An arresting poem of Hennessy's I'm including here first appeared in *Matter*, which I'd never heard of: that was a mood-lightener too. I was delighted to see the venerable *New Republic*'s poetry editor, Rowan Ricardo Phillips, publish so many winners online. I limited myself to reprinting two, one by the distinguished Grace Schulman, the other by a poet previously unknown to me, Natalie Scenters-Zapico. Phillips is represented here by a fine poem of his own in another small but influential journal, *The Threepenny Review*. (Possibly irrelevant disclosure: he's also the author of an entertaining and expert prose book I wish I'd written, about watching a year's worth of televised tennis.)

The shortest poem in the book, the jaunty, three-line "Passion and Form," is by a much-loved poet who can say no more: the 2021 Nobel laureate Louise Glück, who died in the fall of 2023. A long-ish poem, "All Souls," by Saskia Hamilton, who died last summer and whose stanzas showed she knew she had little time, was too moving not to include. There is no entry in this book by David Ferry, splendid poet and translator of poetry, who left us at the heroic age of ninety-nine last November. I do include a poem by Mark Strand, however, who died in 2014. He comes back to life with a "best poem of 2024" because a poem *The New Yorker* had accepted in 1994 was only recently exhumed. The poem is vintage Strand, not least because it contains a meta-frisson: it imagines another dead poet, Strand's favorite, Wallace Stevens, reviving to read his poems at the 92nd Street Y.

If there is any trend in this book, I suppose someone could say I leaned toward longer poems. But only if the poem earned every line! I apologize to readers and writers of prose poetry: you'll find none here, except for one section of Saskia Hamilton's verse poem. I really *was* looking for excellent specimens of the genre, having in mind a standard: Mark Strand's whole book of prose poems, *Almost Invisible*, which is one of my favorite collections of the past twenty-five years. I sense that prose poems have tended to get longer and longer in recent hands, and thus risk losing an essential tool that lineated poems, with the fractional pause given by line breaks, more often achieve: white space and lyric mystery. Long poems have their ways of achieving open-endedness, though. Here you'll find Charles Martin's leisurely but sculpted "You Summon Me . . . ," in which he rhymes "fame" with "*Whatsisname*"; and here is an extended excerpt from Robyn Schiff's book-length poem *Information Desk: An Epic*, about her former job as a staffer answering visitors' questions at the Metropolitan Museum. (The poem is actually about everything, although this section is about cockroaches.) The impressive long poems by Amy Glynn, Jacqueline Osherow, and Matthew Yeager differ in every way except in verve: there's something about a longer form that encourages flights of fancy and varieties of tone. And I can't help praising a thirteen-sonnet sequence that isn't exactly a crown, but resembles it—a nonce form by David Lehman, in which two refrain lines repeat, sometimes with small adjustments, something like a villanelle.

One of the best poets writing in this country, David Lehman has rarely allowed his poems to appear in this series in the thirty-six years he has overseen it. It's good policy, I think, for poet-editors not to choose themselves for publication; but as guest editor, I can't leave out his poem "Ithaca." In fact, these thirteen sonnets that first appeared in *The Hudson Review* are only part of a book-length work, which plays upon modern Ithaca, New York, where the poet lives, and the Ithaca of Ulysses. The poem is about the journey of love and marriage as well as the journey to death, which fortunately takes many detours. "Happy" is a much-repeated word in this poem, and it makes me happy to offer it.

★ ★ ★

One of the younger poets in this anthology, Stephen Kampa, may give me the right note to sign off with. His deliberately brief poem, "Someone Else's Gift," first published in yet another small but mighty journal, *Literary Matters*, seems in conversation with Shakespeare's Sonnet 29, in which even the greatest of poets confesses to "Desiring this man's art and that man's scope." Fretting over such comparisons, Kampa writes,

> Means answering a roguish shout we follow
> Down some smashed-bottle alley to a hollow
> Recess, a doorway, where
> If luck has tailed us on that lonely walk,
> When we knock, because we *have* to knock,
> No one will be there.

No one? Well, perhaps. As Dickinson wrote, "I'm Nobody! Who are you?" Kampa's vision is a scary one, but beautiful because it has been expressed with such uplifting craft. Let's make sure, then, that we ourselves are there when we knock. Let's try to put our own vanities aside when we write poems, and let's read the poems by other people that make us feel most alive. Let's do it simply because we are human.

THE
BEST
AMERICAN
POETRY
2024

KIM ADDONIZIO

Existential Elegy

◊ ◊ ◊

Maybe everyone is walking around thinking something abstract and ontological
like *The existence of others as a freedom defines my situation*

and is even the condition of my own freedom. Maybe de Beauvoir
opens her notebook & writes it as soon as she sits down at the Deux Magots.

Life is inherently meaningless, probably thinks Sartre, across from her at the table,
studying the waiter. The chef savagely prepares a tart for its destruction.

Yet the street lamps blink on without thinking *Light, then nothing . . .*
as the booksellers along the Seine close their metal boxes.

Humming, a woman pulls her damp dress from a basket,
then clothespins her simulacrum to the line.

So maybe not everyone. Maybe I can just lie here on the couch & pet the cat
the rest of the afternoon. He seems troubled

ever since the other one died. He won't chase that snaky rainbow thing
when I drag it over the carpet. What is he thinking? *Snaky rainbow things*

are but fleeting pleasures distracting us from the terror of the void that awaits us?
My first & only time in Paris was thirty years ago. It was February, & snowing.

I wandered Montparnasse cemetery while heady thoughts flurried
from the clouds, wet my face & disappeared. Everyone I loved was still alive.

Paris is still there. The *bouquinistes* too—rare editions & magazines, postcards,
    souvenirs.

The Deux Magots is still there. But now, supposedly, everyone interesting goes
  to the Flore.

Look at them, alive in this poem, holding their menus & about to disappear.
De Beauvoir weeps as Sartre's lowered in.

from *New England Review*

Kyiv

◇   ◇   ◇

I don't believe in poetry
the poet said to the plant
trying hard to be a tree
in the rubble of the city.

I believe in your assembly
the poet said to the sticks of wood
holding up the fragile seedling
like an art piece.

Your form is the future
the poet offered the construction
unaware what that was
saying about it all.

Then the testing of the midnight breeze
and the leaves passed
all that they could
to the poet.

Leaning is a kind of stand
the plant revealed
over and over to the poet
buried in the sidewalk exchange.

A fire hydrant is a kind of fire hydrant
the plant broke down to the poet
trying hard to be a poem
in the rubble of the city.

from *Commonweal*

Amenorrhea

◊ ◊ ◊

The page is blank.
The ark caulked shut.
Lazarus won't get up.
My body, meant to signal every month,
goes dark.
My progeny sit
like passengers in a choppy plane,
both engines out,
their doomed heads tucked between their
knees.
Fetal and in position, they tense
as the plane drops down,
an egg with no membrane
woven to catch it.
Month after month
I neither bleed nor bear.
This woman's barrenness
revives the poet's fear—
the line stops here.

from *Freeman's*

CATHERINE BARNETT

Apophasis at the All-Night Rite Aid

◊   ◊   ◊

Not wanting to be alone
in the messy cosmology
over which I at this late hour
have too much dominion,
I wander the all-night uptown Rite Aid
where the handsome new pharmacist,
come midnight, shows me to the door
and prescribes the moon,
which has often helped before.

from *The Kenyon Review* and *The Best American Poetry Blog*

First Philosophy

◇   ◇   ◇

What is your all-time favorite
phenomenon? Mine is when
the error is as lovely as the aim.

The other day, my wife texts me, *Love
thy baby*, like a contemporary
commandment. Later, she explains

that she meant to write *Love that baby*,
in response to a Mint Condition song
I sent that morning, but I can't let

the first phrase go. It reminds me of those
older saints on Sunday saying *Look at God*
whenever they were interrupted

by transcendent beauty. I tried & did not
see Him, nor dare to ask where I might
search. But I cherished the lesson; took

personally that charge to study the invisible,
call forward its power through chant or speech,
a distinct vocal pattern or arrangement of keys,

& the spirit would cast its fathomless cloak
over us. Make us glow. At home, we worshipped
precision: children honed by hot combs & ironing

boards, perfect grades, our family name
a banner we carried in our war against
the outside world. How did I get here?

This soft blue house in Massachusetts,
my hand against the Japanese maple
outside to better hear its wisdom,

son singing ballads in his toddler Esperanto
downstairs, as I try to compose the story
of our arrival—getting the details wrong,

no doubt, though that melody
is unmistakable, clear—from all those
dreams, dueling, in the air.

from *AGNI*

APRIL BERNARD

"Sithens in a net"

◇   ◇   ◇

from a poem by Sir Thomas Wyatt

What we try to snag and hold fast
of laughter, wood smoke, but especially
the necessary ignorance

to go forward, to trust: I have netted
baubles from air bubbles, pictures of cozy
life in books, the way hot cider

by a warm stove completes winter
and sunset was sunset because you said
"Look at that!" to someone you loved.

At a reading, John Ashbery was asked,
"But what was that *about*?" and he said,
"I guess I'm just sad about time,"

and who can be sorry he was sad, when
such fabric lengths of poems came off
the loom, in down-home-and-I-guess baroque.

Sometimes my dog turns, flops down,
and presses against me with a sigh that
fills the world with peace, making

permanent what would otherwise fly away
on the lash of a clock's tick. You have to think
about things in a different way, allow

ephemera to etch their brain-webs,
allow yourself to last as another beholds.

from *The New York Review of Books*

Miasma

◇ ◇ ◇

The plague's a lot more boring than I thought.
I hide. I wait. I write polemic prose.
Who knows what someone has or hasn't got?

I avoid strangers, do as I was taught.
The Wi-Fi's buffering. The laptop froze.
The plague's a lot more boring than I thought.

It's in a cough, a tasteless patch, a clot,
or nothing, or a swelling of the toes.
Who knows what someone has or hasn't got?

Airplanes are grounded, slots untouched. The hot
dates, the booze, the savings—it all goes.
The plague's a lot more boring than I thought.

My lying foes expose the lies I've bought.
Liars! I hope they end up comatose.
Who knows what someone has or hasn't got?

Refrigerators sputter. Bodies rot.
We slump at screens. Joints harden in the pose.
The plague's a lot more boring than I thought.

The things I used to live for, I do not.
Abstraction breeds inside me. Feeling slows.
Who knows what someone has or hasn't got?
The plague's a lot more boring than I thought.

from *Smartish Pace*

The Deer

◇   ◇   ◇

Walking alone in a forest, I came upon
a deer—this was not a vision.
It faced me, on its four thin legs,
unmoved as a cave painting
brushed by light. I made myself still.
I spoke to it, softly. I can't remember
what I said. It regarded me as a god would,
transfixed by my astonishment.
Then, slowly, I moved closer, and the deer
did not run. By now, you know it was love
I walked toward, not the deer, but
what hung in the space between us. I know
it was love because, as I held
my breath, the deer took
a few steps toward me before
bounding into the camouflage
of branches and leaves.

from *The New York Review of Books*

At Sixty-Five

◊　◊　◊

It was all so different than he expected.
For years he'd been agnostic; now he meditated.
For years he'd dreamed of being an artist living abroad;
now he reread Baudelaire, Emerson, Bishop.
He'd never considered marriage . . .
Still, a force through green *did* fuse.
Yes, he wore his pants looser.
No, he didn't do crosswords in bed.
No, he didn't file for Medicare.
Yes, he danced alone in the bathroom mirror,
since younger men expected generosity.
Long ago, his thesis had been described as promising,
"with psychological heat and the consuming
will of nature." Now he thought, "*This* then is all."

On the rooftop, in pale flickering moonlight,
he pondered the annihilated earth.
At the pond, half-a-mile across was not
too far to swim because he seemed to be going
toward something. Yes, the love impulse
had frequently revealed itself in terms of conflict;
but this was an old sound, an austere element.
Yes, he'd been no angel and so what . . .
Yes, tiny moths emerged from the hall closet.
Yes, the odor of kombucha made him sick.

Yes, he lay for hours pondering the treetops,
the matriarchal clouds, the moon.
Though his spleen collected melancholy trophies,
his imagination was not impeded.

from Poem-a-Day

The Monet Conundrum

◊   ◊   ◊

Is every one of these poems
different from the others
he asked himself,
as the rain quieted down,

or are they all the same poem,
haystack after haystack
at different times of day,
different shadows and shades of hay?

from *Five Points*

Cleptopolitan

◇　◇　◇

In my living room, I have a painting of my living room.

I once got as far as the kitchen of the wrong house.

My wife refuses to call herself an artist which means
her paintings are nobody's business. The one
of the living room was done by someone else.

I have nagging suspicions I've yet to discover.

The most popular street name in America is Park.
The second is Second. After that it's mostly trees
and presidents. The fear of crossing a street has three
different names. I wrote this lying down in a driveway.

When I look at a star, any star, I remember no blade
of grass can keep me here.

My car came with maps to the rest of the country.
Every morning the windshield bears the prints
of some small predator. I look through them
driving to work.

To the best of my recollection I've never fallen asleep.

Today as I pulled up to my house, a man got in the back
and gave me an address. When I told him I wasn't a taxi,
he apologized and got out. I pulled away again and drove
aimlessly.

My wife sleeps like a professional artist.

I've been accused of bias toward robots.

My most frequent dream is about losing my car and then
my clothes. I must search for them naked, all the time
hiding from help. It ends in a park the size of my life.

It's the second page and this poem has a home, a wife,
a car and a job. In the coming months, it will grow
uneasy about its advantages.

My wife is painting a painting already painted.

If this were a children's song, someone would be trapped
inside it as a warning.

In the future, our homes will be inside us.
We'll fill the rooms with art and strangers.

from *Poetry Northwest*

Conscription

◊   ◊   ◊

All the families alike in their unhappiness,
the mother waking early to draw the curtains,
to set out the butter, soon the father sitting glumly
at the head of the table, soon the son come down
dressed in fatigues, his shaved face mirrored on the table,
soon the son dying, all the sons dying: only here
is he still there, it is still dark, the butter is still cold,
the mother's hand paused on the blinds, which fall
slightly apart, a narrow strip of white on the dark floor,
the light's arm on the carpet like a man
reaching to touch his lover's beard.

from *Washington Square Review*

The Remnant

◊   ◊   ◊

Debris spreads like the scattering of bones
on the seabed, coral growing around
the long history of bodies jettisoned.

This is a myth. The artist must
imagine a biblical calamity.
The truth is that, soon, sand will cover
all evidence, soon, even the ancestors
singing deep in the ocean will not
be heard. Soon, in the soft rumble
of walls of water moving,
deafness will be all that is left.

The space beneath the freeway,
all the vehicles emptied, the pillars holding
up the interlocking maze of asphalt
and cement, is the graveyard of all
desire. We will walk among
the broken planks, the empty cars,
the tattered garments, and here
we will find ourselves alone, the wind
moving with the constant hum
of air circling the void.

To hold ourselves intact, we must
close our eyes and imagine green,
and then, for sustenance, drag our
tongues across our foreheads, to taste
the salt and sweet of our hope.

from *The Kenyon Review*

The Bard of Armagh

◇   ◇   ◇

I have aspired to the ease of the drink-steadied harper
        who lives the tune so thoroughly his fast pink hands
dance over the strings like some sharp thing made sharper
        when it's put to use—a family of thing I can't seem to land

on any member of at present, but its heraldic emblem
        pinned behind me like a charm would be the gold cat's paw
chopping cabbage for the supper I'm forever assembling
        on a field of green to set before the Bard of Armagh.

How I love to drift off as I did all through boyhood
        into the daze of my birthright as a person, even if back then
this inwardness felt like thieving liverwurst sandwiches one should
        leave on the platter for the hardworking women, the men

who need all the more to be propped up on the shillelagh
        of animal protein. I myself was satisfied reclining on the straw
I share a name with all afternoon, festooned in the Boyne Valley
        of self-tillage, grazing millennia with the Bard of Armagh.

The sun hums me awake again! Life is over half over.
        Spent in deference, as ever, to those with much more than me.
One can feed their grief or one can cook up ways to cover
        lack over with graciousness. Neither way will set you free

but one will keep you safer put. Death won't embrace me
frowning, or it might—but I heard a tune today, and felt an awe
only we who drift far from shore can, a beauty as if meant to save me
in the currach of its moment, rowed by the Bard of Armagh.

from *Harper's*

Happy End

◇   ◇   ◇

Shh! Rise and be quick about it. Gather your things.

Brother, sister: You were older
but I was the strong one,
humming *one leg, two,*

now socks, now shoes—
all our games lost to shadow.
Just one toy, small. Nothing that rattles.

We knew not to whimper. We set out
where the moon had lain down
a silver rapier,

gravel gnashing its teeth—straight into
the forest they walked us. (Or
were we sent? Either way,

they left or fell back, were simply gone.)
We plucked berries until night
seeped in, soaking the brambles;

the pebbles dropped to mark our trail
stuttering to a stop: *We come this far,*
they whispered.

No crumbs for birdsong, so you sang yourself
towards slumber. I lay down, out of habit,
though there was nothing to see:

The heavens were drowning.
Then suddenly, it was day—
still dreaming, we scrambled up

to greet the dawn, only to face
a line of suns, flashing swirls of red, gold, blue—
I reached for your hand.

This tale was not meant for children,
yet here we were. No other
home expected us. What child

could have resisted such profusion,
the brass-bright proclamation
that someone had found them?

from *Orion*

Irish Traveler's Writer's Block

◊   ◊   ◊

No longer on my knees holed up with a halitosis priest

in the twilit-dark behind a screen of latticed woodwork.

No longer swathed in a fog of incense.

Not thirsting for absolution, but slanting towards a mindset of
confession.

Desire to disclose that mornings I promise myself to write

I do housework, albeit arbitrarily—sprinkling

toilet bowl cleaner as though I'm anointing the sick

but never get around to abrading the porcelain.

Drink two cups of chai, return emails.

Put musk oil in my hair, lemon hydrating lotion on my feet—

a woman just shy of wallpapering her tongue.

I top flaxseed toast with grass-fed butter.

Apply flea and tick repellent to the lonely dogs.

Drape laundry in the coppery sun, tweeze my fading eyebrows.

Put a pot of garbanzo beans on to boil, water the withering fruit trees,

check traps for rotting rodents.

Shake out the Kashmiri prayer rug from under my desk.

Chant mantras in a language not my own.

Only now am I tranquilized down enough to write.

And then Leonard Cohen's lyrics leap into my head:

A million candles burning for the help that never came.

Which sidetracks me into believing it is best *not* to need.

No anodynes or aphrodisiacs, no aide insulating my attic,

no jump when my battery dies, no holy words

or holy water, no cream to temper my caffeine.

Instead of marrying words to trees, I go down the stairs

of my basement, retrieve a polyester superhero costume

to wear to God's funeral. Dab a little perfume

between my breasts and on the small of my back.

I arrive and look around to see who is crying.

I sing burial songs, write my name in the ledger.

Return home, mascara smeared, as if I've been punched

or had a facelift, eat heavily frosted supermarket cake.

Then make an appointment for later the same day,

while I still have tequila in my blood, to get a tattoo

of an invisible rider on the back of a black mare.

from *New Ohio Review*

Avoidance

◊   ◊   ◊

I'm not watching the movie—
just looking up from my book now and then,

puzzled by the actors whispering urgently
as if prompting each other to remember their lines.

If only they would recite the words on the page
in front of me, I'd be more attentive.

Actually, I see I'm doing more than simply
not watching; I am actively avoiding

the film like an unpleasant topic disguised
in furs and jewels. Something about it offends me.

I suppose I could put on a different movie,
but you were sleeping so peacefully,

I didn't want to risk waking you from the lullaby
of this pretentious dated melodrama.

Not only am I busy avoiding the movie,
I am using it as an excuse to avoid continuing

to read the book I had started, which to be honest
isn't so great either. It would seem any activity

one chooses might be motivated by the desire
to get away from something else.

So, I have even physically moved to a different
room. I can still hear the movie, but faintly,

as a kind of spoken music of emotional tones,
and without the visuals, it's almost enjoyable.

I've also put my book down and have begun
writing this poem—obviously the activity

I was avoiding all along, and now can pursue
wholeheartedly to the exclusion of everything else.

from *Court Green*

A Lighthouse Keeper Considers Love

◇   ◇   ◇

She came neither by
schooner nor skiff,
neither by sea nor
brackish channel,
neither by south
nor east, nor west,
and if she came by
north, I saw nothing
of her arrival, standing
as I do with the ice
sheet at my back.
She said neither please
nor thank you,
had neither
suitcase nor hat.
When I gave her
the choice
of spare bedrooms,
she took neither
yellow nor red.
She was neither tired
nor wakeful, spoke
neither kind words
nor cruel. When I set her
a place at my table,
she took neither chair
nor stool. She was neither

pale- nor dark-haired,
neither fat nor thin.
Evenings, I ran her a bath.
She neither got out
nor stayed in.
She could neither dive
to an oyster bed,
nor sail to town
for new oil, nor pull
hard on a fishing line,
nor tell humpback
from right whale.
She was neither
a wit nor a reader,
she could neither
weed nor sow.
When she sat
in the garden
while I pulled
one potato
after another
from a rocky furrow,
she sang
neither fast
nor slow.

from *Guesthouse*

After the Ecstasy, the Laundry

◇   ◇   ◇

—Jack Kornfield, 2001

Window caulk cracking, door padlocked, another laundromat
is closing. How far will people have to drive their dirty
bedspreads? Headlights in daytime, snaking in slow caravans,

black Hefty bags in the backseat, to some suburban strip mall's
Sit and Spin. My years of hoarding quarters, jam-jar maracas
are over. Wheeling my wet load past oversized peepholes

as I eye the red minutes—over. I don't have a private
chapel devoted to laundry as seen on HGTV, just
an "in-unit W/D." And, so must most neighbors. Do I miss

laundromats? Maybe I miss the locker-room-like looking,
the furtive interest surely shared given the rule
to never air. Maybe I miss balling socks, folding

underwear, quickly concealing the crotch, on a long table
where so many strangers' boxers, night gowns have rested.
Any raised surface can be an altar, a place to kneel

side-by-side, mouths open to receive, eyes fixed ahead,
staring into a sleeve. Another laundromat is closing,
and I'm wistful for some imagined leveling, a there-but-

for-the-grace gone, forgetting there's always been drop-off
and laundresses like silent confessors to pound stone, wring
river, inhale the steam of hot metal communing with cotton.

From a stacked dryer in the closet, I carry my tangled
heap to the bed, spilling as I go. Is it lonely? Only
as much as meditation. Fishing and folding, I think:

justice like laundry is never over, which feels profound
until in a bookstore I discover I'm not the first
to find wisdom at the bottom of a hamper. Maybe it's

not how we do it but that we all do, cycling through
the stink and stain of it. An idea so soft from
billions of washings, you can't help wanting to wear it.

from *32 Poems*

DANA GIOIA

Satan's Management Style

◊　◊　◊

I. Punishment in the New Regime

"There are no punishments in Hell except
The hungers and the habits each soul brings.
No medieval dungeons staffed by furies.
You get exactly what you want forever.
What torture more inexhaustible,
So subtle or so slow? But I suspect
The genius of the system's lost on you."

II. *L'Ancien Régime*

"Throughout the aeons demons and the doomed
Collaborated on their punishments—
Each torment tailor-made, almost bespoke.
However awful, it was truly yours.
But population pressure nixed that custom.
It's hard to craft the perfect penalty
With lines of sinners stretching out the door."

III. Management Crisis

"Pity his poor Satanic Majesty,
He was the victim of his own success,
His kingdom mired in pandemonium
With mobs of new arrivals overwhelming
The broken ranks of his bedraggled crew.
The fallen angels were impossible
To manage—even God threw in the towel."

IV. Turnaround

"The Prince of Darkness is a visionary.
Just look at Hell. He took complete defeat
And peddled it as cosmic liberation.
'Profoundest Hell, receive thy new Possessor.
Better to reign in Hell than serve in heaven.'
Pure braggadocio but done with style,
The histrionic swagger demons love."

V. Delegate, Delegate

"Watching the place unravel, Satan saw
An opportunity beyond the chaos.
What if he found a way to let the damned
Punish themselves? They liked to make bad choices.
Why not allow them to repeat their sins?
Let Hell become a game they never win,
A wheel that always hits on double zero."

from *The Hudson Review*

Passion and Form

◊   ◊   ◊

Ah, they have kissed!
The rhyme
Comes in unnoticed.

from *The Threepenny Review* and *Poetry Daily*

Space Is the Final Frontier

◊   ◊   ◊

> *The pattern's partial,*
> *Lord, its pointillism*
> *incomplete: to plot*
> *this form*
> *requires more flame:*
> *this is still*
> *a constellation*
> *without a name.*
> —Richard Kenney

At this point, nothing's truly off the table.
Venus is conjunct Mars in Aries—it's

a gambler's placement. Everything just . . . fits,
however transitory and unstable;

everything's ours and filthy with potential.
Like puzzle pieces, we'll say later, blown

away by how one moment writes its own
little master class on force majeure. Essential

story points emerge in filaments
of glitter: one or two that demarcate

the roofline, or the firmament, intense
enough to see in daylight; then, a great

proliferation littering the field
at dusk. Out of which certain truths emerge,

an archetypal, overwhelming surge
of myth and implication. What's revealed

is, more than anything, a timeless story
of how we conjure meaning from those chance

alignments, accidents of circumstance,
flashes of recognition of a glory

we need to feel has implicated us.
We say *inevitable*, point out the yod

our birth charts share, the thumbprint-divots God
pressed on both our fontanelles at once.

Think of the first time, if you can pin down
what that even was—we were thirteen; we were

infants in San Anselmo; there's a blur
of images from other lifetimes: brown

eyes watching for the slice of light that cuts
the hardwood just before the bedroom door

opens; glass fracturing against the floor
of a room you know but don't; a parakeet's

small riot of green and yellow feathers (whose
pet bird was that? It talked.) Why must it mean

something that I have memories that are
not mine, or that we're haunted by the same

dream where a child with bronze curls says her name
must be spoken? Staggering out of a bar

in Cap Hill, we are dazzled by the cold
clarity of the air, eyes drawn upward by a spate

of brilliances, diamond-cut-diamond spit-
fire daughters of Atlas burning with an old

lament for things that never change, but should.
In eighty-nine years we will meet again,

this time in Jaipur. Me: twelve, over men
already. You: sixteen, shy, with good

teeth and lean thighs and no idea how
to start a conversation. But despite

ourselves we'll share a certain thrill when night
falls and Elektra rises. We will grow

attached. It will seem oddly foreordained.
Things will go sideways anyway. We'll say

it's written. We'll believe it, too. Today
Venus squares Pluto, indicating strained

relations stemming from intensity
of feeling. We do not yet understand

how deep this goes. How could we? One dim strand
emerges. Then, a radiant tapestry.

from *Able Muse*

Each Other Moment

◊ ´ ◊   ◊

We turned location back on.
We were resetting our passwords.
We were scanning the QR code
to order an iced matcha latte.
We were on hold; we were saying
representative into the phone.
We were showing our Excelsior Pass
and putting in our contact information
for timed tickets to the gardens.
We were signing up for a streaming
service and decrying our Zoom
appearance. We were skimming
not reading. We were trawling
and scrolling. We were calculating
the millennia before reefs could
revive and species come back
in colors we haven't imagined.
We were guilty, and each other
moment, also innocent. We were
meditating so the unforgiving
might give a little. We were trying
to find the contact information
for the company. We were
wondering where to recycle
foam rubber. We were listening
to a podcast and downloading
a playlist. We cross-indexed our
top issues in Charity Navigator.

We were making suggested
go bags and stay bins for the likely
floods and fires. We were
wondering why men only
gave us one star. We looked to
the sky for how to help any
anything at all. We hit retweet
on the full moon and we liked
the Big Dipper. Constellations
etch-a-sketched the night, then the
window shade's round pull
rose into a sun and light came on.
We agreed with the ancients;
that was hopeful. We turned location
back off. We were innocent but
each other moment we were lost.

from *Alaska Quarterly Review*

Voyage

◇   ◇   ◇

The ship was crammed to bursting:
luggage, lifejackets, jammed benches,
passengers sitting on one another's laps.
Was this a ferry plying between islands?
We have passed Age's icy caves
And Manhood's dark and tossing waves
And once these were behind us,
we hugged a coast, and glided
past promontories, cliffside villages,
steep hills slanting down to little harbors.
On each pier a festive group was gathered:
bridal whites, bright bouquets,
black suits and glossy patent leather shoes,
vivid even from a distance,
gleamed in the salty air.
A wedding or a festival?
A mourning or a funeral?
The gathered celebrants in every harbor
waved as we sailed past, and we waved back,
steadily plowing onward. Where and when:
not the right questions. Time
was an element, not a place,
and in and through it on we went,
the landmarks of each life
bobbing in our wake.

from *Literary Matters*

All Souls

◇ ◇ ◇

*

Chemical burring of the tongue.
Good to be on the other side
of treatment for now.

We scroll on. Would a codex restore
the balance of recto and verso.

Take up the book. Dreams luminous
in anticipation of the alarm.
When it comes, how dark and modest waking is.

*

Reading the news, waiting for sleep or the night to pass, tap of rain on the window unit, desk of unfinished work in the next room. X the painter has died. Images in my hand of the enormous faces she painted, the cause of death in narrative paragraphs, all the world of representation compressed on the screen.

Why retell the stories of those before us? They already spoke them, or held their tongues—fell silent. A lifetime to overcome the prohibition not to. But the lens is all wrong these days. I'd thought it a sunset, a sketch, told again as all sunsets are. To say something sincerely yet inauthentically is the danger. And Eliot struck "Ode" from the first U.S. edition of his poems to prevent his mother from seeing it. . . .

What prompted that thought? Body does not want to sit up just yet.
One two one two go the taps. The child stirs—light herewith emitted
in the dark.

★

In search of a medicinal hour. Hortus:
sitting at the café with apple cake
while garden-goers stir the gravel path.
Compacted here, luxuriant trained growth
of teaberry, gentian, trumpet vine,
comfrey, field restharrow, &c.
Our apothecary ancestor with his *liber ingressus*
token entered here to gather the herbs
for infusions that were to aid the unwell
caught in the far gone far alone glance
of mortality, moving the clock hands
from one hour into the hour.
Who is there now to announce the triumph
of hope? But by and by, after
seeds have been scattered, stirred and covered over,
blossomed, gathered, dried, crushed. Hot, late afternoon,
bees crossing bees and white butterflies.

★

"Death closes all." Yes. But were they granted
anything, none know beforehand,
breath going out for a decade,
returning in a century,
while those gathered there fall out of
their own pockets, or is it
the count and rhythm, unable
to fix a mark or a lover's thought
at the moment when the face of the encounter
became knowledge completed.

from *The Yale Review*

A Message from Tony Hoagland

◇　◇　◇

I got an email from Tony just now
though he's been dead for a year and a half,
and in the instant before my rational brain
told me it was spam, I felt the thrill
of seeing his name pop up in my in-box,
the dopamine rush that he was writing me
from beyond the grave. And when I clicked
on his name to open the message, the body
of the email consisted only of my first name
followed by an exclamation mark
(as though he was excited to be writing me)
and, under that, a compressed link
in the electric blue that indicated
it was live. My giddy finger slid
the cursor over it, to see what Tony
was sending me—maybe instead of
infecting my computer with malware
that would harvest my data and require me
to pay a huge ransom in cryptocurrency,
the link would take me to a web page
where I could find all the poems
Tony has written since he died.
I paused a moment and thought about
what those poems would be like,
but my imagination failed me. Then
I clicked "delete," and went into my trash

and deleted the message again,
which made me feel timid and puny,
as though, like D. H. Lawrence
and his snake, I'd missed my chance
with one of the lords of life.

from *New Ohio Review*

How to Fold

◇   ◇   ◇

Seated alone at the edge of the bed
grasp the finest fabric first,

the shrunken sock or silk softest to touch
among laundry high & hot enough

to wreathe your body in rags & towels
and undivided multicolor trappings.

When you find your phantom lover's
item in the pile, you will have to decide

how to handle it. When it is an undergarment,
you may grasp the heat

which does not linger in silk or lace.
When it is a shirt or pair of jeans, position

the fabric on your skin in the absent
lover's position. Most of your armor is cotton.

You may undress & lie with the item
against the most exposed part of your seams,

a root work of threads like veins.
The scent folded into the fabric may no longer be

detectable to the unknowing nose.
Folded on the bed alone, conjure the love

under some fabricated light streaming
into the room, a milk-blue ink

at some temperatures, a lucid plasma,
a pearl on the bud & palette in others.

Place your fingers as the fingers are placed.
The oblivious spirit folds out of its material.

Washed till worn, then worn despite tatters.
Fold the legs & arms

until the figure fits neat as a book
of matches in a drawer. The map inside & out

is a mix of missteps & crossroads
bordering cliffs & edges. You cannot live

without the heat & iron of love.
The scent folded into the material travels

as far as music. The scent is like lavender
if lavender were meat-salted & emitting

a heat that travels as far as music.

from *The New York Review of Books*

JOHN HENNESSY

Domestic Retrograde

◇ ◇ ◇

The hummingbird hovered in the kitchen, wrong
side of the door, thudded the glass, stopped

all talk. Our boys drew at the table. I chopped
garlic at the counter. You filled wineglasses

near the sink. The bird in place, everyone
still. More fish swimming the damp June air

than god of war striking a wall, stoking
its foundry of anger and desire—helmeted, snake-

waving Huitzilopochtli, one of your subjects,
devotions, however ironic, maybe half, maybe

less. Wings nearly invisible, a crucifix hologram,
posture held static, petitioning, priestlike, green

back, black and red throat, hardly
the reincarnated warrior, syncretic Mars—

the wars were elsewhere, Donbas, Libya,
Afghanistan, elsewhere, far from our kitchen.

And then everyone moved. I billowed a tea
towel, some Sifnian souvenir, Apollonian

sunburst, gently covered the bird mid-air,
asked you to open the door, in one motion he was

liberated, flying back to the feeder. I wanted you
to love me. I could calm, pacify Mars. I thought

I did it for you. Before the war came
to us, before I knew we were fighting it.

from *Matter*

Pando's Grove

◇   ◇   ◇

In principle, aspen groves are immortal.

So many rescued were turned into trees.
        Daphne into a laurel, Myrrha nursing
her baby on a sweet band of cambium

and, even though I didn't see aspens
        branching above me or hear the wind
ripple through their leaves' ragged teeth,

as I breathed they murmured inside me,
        greening my lungs with their whispers
and gossip. Is it so hard to believe

that I wanted to be what they made of me?—

a seedling born of roots
        the grove set to bind itself together,
clone of a single spawning tree;

that I wanted to wear this bark,
        these branches coated with antlers'
velvet and lichens' mustardy dust:

eyes, lips, tongue gone to mosses,
        seep of springs at my feet, roots
fanning out to the far edge of memory.

from *Southern Indiana Review*

Lamb

◊ ◊ ◊

I had a lamb I brought everywhere

Who only had one eye.

At the train stations,

All the grown-ups would say, be mindful

Of your things, little boy,

Someone will steal right out of your pocket

Or take the watch off your wrist.

My dad had a beautiful overcoat.

The lamb's white fur got smudged.

My brother was a baby,

And in the restaurants,

The old waiters would pick him up

And kiss him again and again on the cheek

With their mustaches

And tell my parents

That they promised they would bring him back in a minute

But now they needed to show the chef.

I don't remember when the eye became unglued

And who knows where it went.

On long train rides,

I remember falling asleep,

Putting my finger in the hole where it used to be.

Once he had to go in an overhead bin,

And he was freezing when I kissed him again.

from Poem-a-Day

MARIE HOWE

Chainsaw

◇ ◇ ◇

There's always a chainsaw somewhere,
the high whine of a drill, somebody building something or
tearing it down, fastening metal to metal.

Almost everywhere the sound of the human will,
the bluster of an engine, the grind of a blade, the wheel,
hammering, repair.

Someone nailed to a cross, someone leashed, lashed.
Someone hung from a scaffold: listen: the squeak of the rope:
more hammering.

Kill him with his own gun, one woman shouted, *Kill him with his own
gun.*

What have we made? What are we making?
And who or what made us that we should make such things as we do
and did?

We grow smaller—we break things,
then turn to each other and beg for what no human can give.

from *Poetry*

Closure

◇　◇　◇

My parents were scheduled to divorce on Valentine's Day.
I was there in the beginning, sat next to my grandmother,

in her teal blue dress and hot combed strands. As a rule,
she refused to appear unrefined. In a warm church in Trinidad,

a wedding evening in hurricane season, we wore our Sunday best,
my mother and I, in matching white lace and wide eyes.

Why shouldn't this bond be marked by an angel with an arrow,
tasked to put an end to the sorrow of suffering alone

love meant to be shared. The sugar apples of my mother's cheeks,
rouged more than the red carnation pinned to my father's smokey

blue suit. I search his handsome jaw and boyish grin for clues. We keep
the happy secrets of these fleeting Trade winds, in the family album,

so old, the memory and the artifact have become one. Pigment sealed
to plastic for eternity, a reality that cannot be undone or loosened,

only destroyed. Marriage is a valentine that misses me
though I have imagined myself able to walk up the aisle,

if not back down it, which is partly why I am disappointed
when the court rescheduled without a reason. Perhaps

the judge on the docket, newly in love, refused to chance the karma
of divorce court. I can say it now, these years later,

I was eager to be asked to witness our legal dissolution.
The annihilation of vows that were broken. Tell me

what's louder: the pluck of the arrow, or the bang of the gavel,
or the everlasting gaze of the firstborn daughter.

from *Guernica*

Japan

◇   ◇   ◇

My brother died in Japan. Each day his voice
on the phone is a wall with a voice in it.
He says he won't go to the Japanese hospital.
He says you don't understand what this is like.
He says I can't breathe.
Everyone has a childhood that kills itself.
When my brother weeps on the phone
I ask him to go on drugs. I ask him to go
to the hospital, dying. At some point
everyone kills a brother with nothing
in his hand. My brother is a monk
who lives on memory the way a sailor
lives on blue and salt. Everyone has a brother
who hangs up. Everyone has a god
with siblings turned against him.
There is no hospital and no drugs.
My brother's ex-wife won't speak to him.
Everyone has an everyone who won't speak
to him. We're all salt and memory, but I can't
say this. I ask my brother not to die in Japan.
Everyone has an ex-wife who is a drug.
My voice is a wall with a voice and I don't know what
this is like. My brother says he wants to play
piano and violin and ride a bicycle on summer roads.
I think we can have a beautiful life, if you'll save me,
my brother says to the wall with the voice in it.
My brother died in Japan. We can have animals
and pianos. We can have land.
Everyone's ex-wife hangs up. Everyone has a summer
that dies in a brother.

from *Conduit*

Byzantine Chanting

◊ ◊ ◊

I could barely catch a single sacred word
The cantor was singing, if you can call that low,
Liturgical droning, or on-and-off sobbing, singing.

His lectern was marble, and opposite the choir.
His singing robes were golden as Arion's,
And swayed in shimmering rhythm to every murmur

He made as he rocked back and forth with his eyes closed.
Like Arion, our master singer had crossed an ocean—
But not on the back of a dolphin (my favorite myth).

His songbook was always open, but never consulted.
Its gilded pages were thick as The Yellow Pages.
My parents bowed their heads when the *psáltis* chanted.

They told us he came from Smyrna when he was small
And the houses were set on fire. Our *psáltis*, reciting
The Psalms of Exodus he learned as a child.

And here he was, in Lynn, Massachusetts, when Lynn
Was known as "Shoe City." But all I could see
In all that chimney smoke was smoldering Smyrna.

Even on Sundays the smell of factory leather
Hung in the air, as pungent as incense, until
We entered church and heard the cantor's voice.

Whatever Byzantium meant in Byzantine Greek,
I studied the sagging jowls of that refugee's face
As he chanted the rising and falling cadences.

Just down the street, six days a week, our *psáltis*
Was flaying hides that soaked in bubbling vats.
But as long as his singing robes were swaying, I pictured

Leaping dolphins, and worn-out sandals crossing the desert.

from *Raritan*

Someone Else's Gift

◊   ◊   ◊

Always to long for someone else's gift—
To blow that blistering alto sax, to lift
    Into the flash-bulbed air
For a reverse slam dunk while stunned guards gawk,
To have a punster's cheek or porn star's cock,
    To capture, share by share,
Gold-plated Wall Street fame, to meditate
Beyond nirvanic depths or radiate
    Beatitudes of prayer
Like any frescoed saint, even to make
A perfect triple-decker dark-fudge cake
    Or master the éclair—
Means answering a roguish shout we follow
Down some smashed-bottle alley to a hollow
    Recess, a doorway, where
If luck has tailed us on that lonely walk,
When we knock, because we *have* to knock,
    No one will be there.

from *Literary Matters*

Self's the Man

◊   ◊   ◊

How is it we can know that there's a word
when we can't for the life of us think of it? My word—
worse—who's the Oz-like Dream Master
who casts my dream to its catastrophe?
Who is that shaper of the unforeseen?
Here in my hemispheres, are we a foursome?
Dog-faithful, some insomniac Man-Friday
shook me gently at five sharp last Friday.
Why? I had to catch an early flight.
Who's *he*? Say, is that faithful acolyte
who recognizes four is two-plus-two—
who rings the bell to signal something's *true*—
the same as that valet who ties my shoes?
It's my *Unconscious Mind*? Excuse me, whose?
Who carries words up from the basement, rung
by rung, depositing them on my tongue
in the nick of time, as though I "thought of them?"
That's what I think, of course. "I thought of them."

from *The Hopkins Review*

Kiss Me Deadly *(1955)*

◇   ◇   ◇

Dr. G. E. Soberin, dubious apothecary, torturer,
   is handy with a pair of pliers or truth serum.
      Wearing pinstriped suits, he has a sideline
      trading a cube of nuclear Armageddon.
Velda calls it "the great whatsit," done in leather
with two straps like the sample case of a vendor,
      cracked open smiling on a glimpse of doom

that sighs and raves, its celluloid radiance
      a mutation of the genre, a kind of isotope,
         the director's knuckle-sandwich cynicism
         pummeling the film's romantic fatalism,
noir lit by the light of a thousand suns,
being Trinity's light and the MacGuffin's,
      until there's nothing left but a bloody pulp

and an ancient curiosity. *At the gates of hell,*
      listen to me as if I were Cerberus who barks,
         says Dr. Soberin. *Whoever looks at Medusa is*
         changed, not into stone, but brimstone and ashes.
What's in this box can't be divided, Gabrielle.
You should have been called Pandora. I will tell
      you where to take it. But don't . . . don't open . . . the box.

It's a meltdown, a *real* meltdown, of modern society,
      and it all plays out in a little bungalow
         between Zuma and Point Dume on Westward Beach,
         being as likely a place as any for such
a reversion, a dissolution into spiritual degeneracy
as Mike Hammer and Velda stumble into the primordial sea
      and THE END crawls up to fill each glaring window.

from *The New Criterion*

My Brothers, the Olmec

◊ ◊ ◊

You came by woven reed boats
    forced across angry water
    driven by mighty winds.

Or a swift long skiff ferried you
    here by twenty-four oarsmen,
    twelve on each side, six front

& rear, powered by the rotation
    of two shifts, all twenty-four
    who tugged along dreamwork

on waves. They rowed around
    sun & moon setting & rising,
    inhale & exhale, all as one

song of the whole crew rotating,
    pushing ahead until they saw
    green land, their oars parting

blue rhythms of what's to come
    or being born on the other side
    of the world. Yes, my brothers,

you of bittersweet herbs & chants
    taken in sea breeze, what secrets
    & taboos, myths, laws, & oaths

did you bring here? I believe it was
    your laughing, thundering voices
    in the drums. Where did you hide

those days of wild cats, serpents,
      & plots? Did you arrive out of
      nowhere, always here, stout

& tall, hewn of stone miles away,
      but now rooted into green earth?
      Mystery how you rose or sprung

up, somehow you became almost
      another people, calling windswept
      sea waves at your strong backs.

If you were always here, brothers,
      you wouldn't have danced feet
      bloody under a full moon. No,

the charts were blue-black skies,
      but not to worship hidden icons
      before & beyond, & you cannot

walk hilly paths home any longer.
      How did they capture you in
      solid stone rolled into a green

valley? Yes, that's right—rolled!
      But first stones were rounded.
      No, sacred work is never easy.

My Olmec brothers, I saw you
      with my own eyes, true & dark,
      in the Museum of Archaeology

of Mexico City, tall & righteous,
      & I love the red-hot peppers
      baked into your maize bread.

from *Poetry*

from Ithaca

◇ ◇ ◇

> *Heureux qui, comme Ulysse, a fait un beau voyage.*
> —Joachim du Bellay

1.

Happy as Ulysses is he who ventures forth,
who leaves behind his idols and his homeland
and mourns the loss of his mariners
shamed like hogs under a witch's spell
or swallowed whole by a one-eyed colossus and yet
he opposes the wind with his beard of sea salt
after one more failure clinging to a spar.
And the poor cottage of an October oracle,
with leaves burning in the distance of a miracle,
absent the flames and amber lights eternal,
is as dear to him as the hospital bed he left
on the appointed day, walking the whole way,
quickening his stride as if he were sprinting
like a sandaled youth past the lotus-tempted sailors.

2.

What did he believe in? God—or nothing,
which didn't amount to the same thing.
There was love, and there was lovemaking,
the stuff of collegiate heartbreak morphed
into a porn classic by a French libertine
writing under the pen name Tiresias
still thirsty for sacrificial blood in Hades
quizzed by nobody special going to Ithaca.

What he wants is to return to the fork
in the road forty years ago. What he gets
are directions: "You can't miss it."
In a soundproof room, walled with cork,
he hears the song, has no regrets.
If he sees her face, he will kiss it.

3.

What did he believe in? He thought about it,
puffed on his pipe, emptied the ashes,
refilled the bowl, lit it, puffed again,
said "yeah" and blew out the match.
But then as he puffed some more he
refused to choose between death as
oblivion on the one hand and immortality
on the other, and furthermore doesn't
the immortal as opposed to the permanent
exist as merely a poem: a lovely, glorious nothing
that a young man crafted at three
in the morning to woo a young woman
whose name he cannot recall now that
sixty winters are on his head and hers?

4.

What did he believe in? Marriage, she said,
changing the subject. He carried the ladder
painted the hall changed the oil in his truck
fixed the leak, wiped his brow, sipped
tea with rum and lemon juice and napped
with the light on, a book open on his lap,
as the day waned and his wife prepared
a special dish for him, though he is nothing
more than a functionary, a low-level diplomat
negotiating the next war. One is always
on the way. The man walks home
from work, a familiar mile of drug stores
and butchers, and then, quickening,
he sees the lights on in the top-story flat.

5.

Happy the man who voyages in the vanguard
with crazed mariners, reluctant prophets,
compulsive liars and tale-tellers, as the flask
of brandy is passed from hand to hand
and the tobacco smoke fills the air like an arena
in a black-and-white movie about brawlers
from the Bronx and guys who fixed the fights.
Happy the worker on Friday nights
and the woman singing of her sorrow
and her lust for Ulysses tied to the mast
who hears the longing that matches his own.
What does he believe in? Yesterday,
but a yesterday that has not yet come to pass
or to grief, like his naive belief in the gods at play.

6.

What does he believe in? God.
The torturer smiled. God? Which god?
The god who argued with Abraham,
who tempted Abraham and spared Isaac,
who wrestled with Jacob and gave Joseph
the power to interpret dreams? Or the god
who blessed the meek forsaken by his father?
He smiled sadistically. Enjoy your cigarette
and your shot of scotch, he said. You believe
in lucid days and ludic nights,
in words, wine talons, water-lights,
the fog in the fir trees.
You will know death to the bone—
the climate of the grave.

7.

What does he believe in? He believes
envy is to the present as hypocrisy was to
fashionable Parisians in 1855. He believes
we are better off in calculable ways yet

guilt remains the constant in the equation
and nothing reeks of meaning like Crusoe's
unused knife on the dresser. His collections
amuse him yet days go by without them.
But shelves he cannot pass without staring
at the spines of the books he read in college
and can still recite their openings (*The Trial*,
The Good Soldier, *The Birth of Tragedy*) and
endings: the happy major's "Hot dog!",
the kids shouting "Hurrah for Karamazov!"

8.

Happy the hero who, like Ulysses,
heeds the voice of the reckless sea
and survives the loss of his crew because
the gray-eyed goddess of wisdom
sees herself in his eyes. Happy the man
who heard what no other mortal heard
and saw what others have only
dreamed they have seen. Happy
the athlete in the sunlight though he
will die young and the chapter will end
with the man who gets on the bus and
believes that at the end of the journey
he will reach home in time for the toasts
to his absence and his rivals' empty boasts.

9.

What did he believe in? Biology,
anatomy, and the destiny of all creation
which admits of no exception
to the slow decay of time
or the rapid route to the underground;
in the dead vast and middle of the night
with no pain or with a surfeit of fright.
Happy the hero who worries less
about his mistress's unholy mattress.
Happy as Ulysses on completing

his journey in Ithaca is he after
a lifetime of fake cheer and cheating
in an upper-story office on Liberty Street,
an easy walk from the A train.

10.

Each sunset stayed for its allotted time.
The darkness came on as if someone threw a switch.
What did he believe in? The darkness.
But was there anything behind or beyond it?
The question bothered him, but the hours he spent
in the fifth-floor conference room had taught him
to suspend the discussion while sitting on committees
charged with judging the work of other committees
or in mindless crowds cheering for the underdog
in a game whose rules he barely understands
or chatting up the woman in the gray pencil skirt
at the gallery opening of the sunset show
with a y-shaped glass full of her orange scent
and the afterglow of gin chilled to bone zero.

11.

What did he believe in? the death of god
announced by a syphilitic madman
on the radio for servicemen abroad
at halftime after the benedictions and anthems.
It was futile but could no more be resisted
than an old man's wish to be young but she
interrupted his reverie. What about me?
All right, he said, accepting the tea, the jam,
the toast, the lemon, and the bowl of sugar.
I'll bite. What do you believe in? She ate
a biscuit before answering. In you, of course.
You're the only thing I believe in. You're
a beautiful liar, he smiled. But I love thee,
and when I love thee not, chaos is come again.

12.

Happy the man who cultivates the illusion
that he believes in nothing
but the curative powers of the summer sun
and the pleasures of the mind
as he contemplates performing one last work
of noble action before the ban on books begins.
Happy the fellow who walks the city streets,
infiltrates the crowd, leaves messages for
strangers to read later, runs on anxiety,
a cloud of unknowing protecting him.
He knows what to do if someone shouts fire.
The go-go ego prohibits lamentation
for object loss in childhood, fear of castration
in the phallic period, dread of the superego's ire.

13.

What does he believe in?
He believes in lateness.
He arrived late last night.
He came to his senses too late
to recover anything or rescue anyone
from the burning house.
He watched it burn from the road.
He believes that a genius lived here
in a room exactly like his
with a window overlooking
an array of pines some deer and a lake
with some lights twinkling on the rocks,
and he is writing these words
in this room in the burning house.

from *The Hudson Review*

ADA LIMÓN

In Praise of Mystery:
A Poem for Europa

◇   ◇   ◇

Arching under the night sky inky
with black expansiveness, we point
to the planets we know, we

pin quick wishes on stars. From earth,
we read the sky as if it is an unerring book
of the universe, expert and evident.

Still, there are mysteries below our sky:
the whale song, the songbird singing
its call in the bough of a wind-shaken tree.

We are creatures of constant awe,
curious at beauty, at leaf and blossom,
at grief and pleasure, sun and shadow.

And it is not darkness that unites us,
not the cold distance of space, but
the offering of water, each drop of rain,

each rivulet, each pulse, each vein.
O second moon, we, too, are made
of water, of vast and beckoning seas.

We, too, are made of wonders, of great
and ordinary loves, of small invisible worlds,
of a need to call out through the dark.

from The Library of Congress website and NASA's Europa Clipper website

Shopping Lists

◊   ◊   ◊

I use Google Translate for the shopping lists
from V, a friend in Ukraine.
Nappies, baby milk, medical staplers, burn gel,
intubation tubes (no size specified),

a little like the shopping lists from the President—
multiple rocket launch systems, Grad, Uragan,
tanks (T-72, either the American or German analogs),
air defence systems. No kidding.

Today V writes, "Thank you! We are together!"
And on his Facebook page—here Google takes over
as they take over everything—I'll do the line breaks:

The image can be: 1 person and text
found killed hands were tied
with an iron cable blackened body—

Oksana applied on clothes and special signs
now the body is under examination in Fastov

I look on the person's page. A recent post
details another
shopping list, a list of goods sent home
from the Kyiv region
by a Russian soldier
to his wife. Coffee grinder,
microwave ovens, TVs,

in 17 parcels.
Total weight, 440 kg.

I'm sitting on the balcony,
drinking coffee in the sunlight
619 miles from V.

Google Maps makes taking the trip
seem a perfectly sane
and logical thing to do.

It would take me 13 hours and 21 minutes.

from *AGNI*

Charmed Life

◇   ◇   ◇

Destiny blessed me. Kismet kissed me.
Accident aimed, but the meteor missed me.
Fate did me favors. Luck had my back
For a leisurely picnic between the tracks.
Joy was a contract I printed and inked.
How could I know
In the mountaintop snow
Nemesis tiptoed behind me and winked?

from *Literary Matters*

Weather Conditions

◊   ◊   ◊

Meteorologist says "For your local weather,

here is a quick peek out your window."

You look: you see houses leaning against one another for support—

as if the whole world is falling apart.

On a front porch a woman is breastfeeding a newborn and

you know a pointless war rages on, on the other side of the river.

You see that poor beggar-family with a little boy

walking along the winter beach. You see the retired general

going to the bar for his morning coffee.

Using your binoculars, you see through the window

of the watering hole a shivering couple huddled together

at a table in the corner. Two tables away, the circus performers

enjoying a morning pick-me-up, but you don't see the weather.

from *The New Yorker*

You Summon Me . . .

◊   ◊   ◊

1/

You summon me from silence like a Muse,
And without even asking, freely use
        The form I made my own, my *Rubáiyát*,
On any subject matter that you choose!

2/

As if dependency somehow defined you,
You don't appear to mind me here behind you
        And seem to find a shelter underneath
The shadow of my reputation! Mind you,

3/

I'm not displeased to see this new employment
Of my old quatrain, this fine-tuned toy, meant
        To be used for the simultaneous
Delivery of wisdom and enjoyment.

4/

Nor do I reckon that my man FitzGerald—
Edward, not Scott—has been at all imperiled
        By what you've done already, or are doing:
Though minor, Fitz is permanently laureled.

5/

The one who brought me everlasting fame
Deserves to have his share of the acclaim
        He hungered for and in part came to know,
Though now he's largely known as *Whatsisname*.

6/

Let others argue whether he construed
My meanings with as little latitude
      As a translator should: I see now that no
Translation is devoid of attitude.

7/

As for *your* purposes, which may appear
Pointless to some—or many, as I fear—
      Objections are no longer mine to make,
For reasons which I'll presently make clear.

8/

You follow one who followed my design
And imitate an imitation? Fine:
      Whatever feathers you are like to ruffle,
Or hours you'll have wasted, aren't mine;

9/

I was already an established brand
Who had no further craving to expand
      His empery @ *copyrightKhayyam*:
I did enough to generate demand,

10/

And saw no point in writing more, since whether
I did or not, more quatrains would foregather
      Under the great umbrella I had raised:
Write them myself? Let others have the bother!

11/

The problem by which we are most perplexed,
We serial purveyors of the text,
      Is that, while so few will have read our latest,
All show such lively interest in our next:

12/

"We hope you're hard at work now on some vast
New epic which will leave your peers outclassed
      Completely, and will shower you with prizes—"
—You haven't cut the pages on my last,

13/

The one that even friendly critics spurned:
"At some point, one would think he would have learned
      To do it better . . ." "Or to give it up . . ."
Of the five copies sold, three were returned.

14/

Didn't that happen to poor dotty Fitz?
I can't recall exactly now, but it's
      No matter, really: any writer's life
Will separate a fellow from his wits!

15/

So whether I wrote a little or a lot,
Or if I wrote it all or wrote it not,
      Matters to none at all, including me,
The famous author of the *Rubáiyát*.

16/

The candle lasted longer than the game,
As countless bards dissembled in my name,
      Some quite like me, but others not so much—
Theirs was the labor, mine was the acclaim!

17/

Each of their poems consisted of just four
Lines in Iambic 5, and not one more,
      With each of them rhyming A-A-BLANK-A;
But never was there ever such a corps

18/

Of diverse piglets at a single teat.
"Variety" just doesn't cover it:
      I was, as I had never been before,
A multitude: Omar, *Omas*, Omit.

19/

Once all the weakest had been winnowed out,
By editors who have been known to shout,
      "He never could have written lines that bad,
That isn't his, it can't be, I've no doubt!"

20/

That last one there might *not* be mine in fact:
Although they are, as usual, exact,
      The rhymes are really much more *meh* than *me*,
The kind that lesser poets all attract.

21/

Even today no lack of talent bars
A mighty host of wannabe Omars
      From cranking out quatrains they claim are mine:
As far from mine as mine are from the stars!

22/

Sorry! I'd no intention to suggest
That you're just as immodest as the rest.
      If I may go on, this led to some confusion,
This multitude of cuckoos in my nest.

23/

Was I an orthodox Mohammedan
Or sceptic of the atheistic clan;
      A Sufi whirling in the outer reaches,
Or Greek-inflected epicurean,

24/

A moony sybarite, always in love?
Push, as it happened, never came to shove:
      I never had to choose just one of them,
Being, as one is, most of the above.

25/

The last thing that we should expect to find
In any poet is a single mind:
      Just pick up any poem that you see,
Whether it's metrical or the other kind,

26/

And clap it to your ear: a disordered rout
Of voices whisper, mumble, whine, and shout,
      Competing—for what else is authorship?
To see if one can drown the many out.

27/

So having other poets first immerse
Themselves in my work and then write my verse
      Was just a sound career move on my part—
If poets can be said to *have* careers.

28/

For in this echo chamber of a form,
A plethora of voices is the norm:
      "Who owns this work?" "Is it original?"
Are questions better put to bees aswarm.

29/

Did you write that? Did Fitz? Or is it mine?
At this point our voices intertwine,
      And none of us can claim sole ownership
Of an errant stanza or stray line.

30/

Yet all of us have been brought up to count
Originality as paramount,
    The *sine qua non* of the creative act—
Unlikely that without it you'll amount

31/

To much at all—you surely won't ascend
Unto the upper ranks of the high end
    Creatives, will you? Well, if you're just not
Original, can't you at least pretend?

32/

But if you're still there listening to me,
And odd as it may seem, you seem to be,
    You will have long anticipated this:
Forget about originality,

33/

As far back as you go, you cannot reach
The first word trembling on the verge of speech,
    Already luminous with all that follows;
And if the past connects us each to each,

34/

Originality means doing what
Was done already by some other mutt
    Who's imitating in his turn another:
"Originality is nothing but

35/

Judicious imitation," says Voltaire,
Who pauses for a moment with the air
    Of one almost expecting a response,
Before he pivots to descend the stair.

36/

So leaving us with nothing left to say,
Our *philosophe* has made his getaway,
    Counting on our fumbling attempts
At vanquishing *l'esprit de l'escalier,*

37/

Which translates into "What I shoulda said . . ."
A useful phrase, when all your hopes are dead,
    Or you've just mumbled, "Thanks for a real nice time,"
And are returning to an unshared bed.

38/

The Big Bang went entirely unheard,
The epigrammatist had the last word,
    And in between, the muddled middle beckons
To those of us at home in the absurd;

39/

Using the worn-out tools that you have come by,
As well as those that you yourself supply
    From your own toolkit, do as you are able
To keep it going; your inability

40/

And the likelihood that you will be forsaken,
Are unimportant here, are to be taken
    For granted when what only matters is
The dialogue with others you awaken.

from *The Hudson Review*

Two Widows, Making a Bed

◇　◇　◇

Look at this! What a wonder
to find it by accident, under the covers
and out of its box.

It's equipped for some duty
to judge by its crankshaft, the structure's
a beauty—I bet that it walks.

Turn it on—can you find any
switch for ignition? They haven't designed many
I'd like to keep. It should rise, it should shine,

it should take a position,
not kill our ambition
or put us to sleep.

Does it sit? Can it stand?
(It has spin, it has spyware—
its handles aren't mangled, so

why does it lie there?!) With stir-stick
and fur trick, a can that's a zinger—could it
just be a man? (Look, it won't lift a finger!)

It's ruthlessly useless. That paltry display
will not come to its senses. And won't
go away. It's enragingly loath

to engage on demand! If it's
this hard to start, then we
never could pause it.

Just give me
a hand. It can go
in the closet.

from *The Hopkins Review*

from Couplets

◇　◇　◇

Her job was taking other people's prose and coaxing
it to coherency. Mine was coaching

young people to translate life experience
to prose. But our own story made no sense

to me and twisted up whenever I tried
writing it. On the bus ride

to her building, I listened to Liz Phair,
Irma Thomas, and an outfit from Montclair

that she and I both loved, of a genre
halfway between emo and Americana,

like the lovechild of Bright Eyes and Loretta Lynn.
So much from that time is still so redolent

of nervousness and sex—her sandalwood cologne
and reading H.D. on her phone,

and crying in the mezzanine
at BAM and on a bench in Fort Greene

Park, and the sticky Ottolenghi cake we made ("no butter"),
and juices from an app. Rebecca West. The comforter

we patched to stop it drowning us
in goose-down every night. Soylent. Cunnilingus.

Saraghina, before all the Sturm und Drang.
The quaver in her voice when she first sang

the song that afterward became
the anthem of our romance, named

after a book of letters named after a fervid,
almost painful shade of red.

★

That fall, I'd rush out of her bed to catch
the seven o'clock train to the college

I taught composition at—
supporting claims, active voice, citation format.

The difference between *summary* and *analysis*
was a large part of the syllabus,

so much so you could say the line between
them was the joist on which the whole semester leaned.

I think I really liked the teaching,
with its emphasis on logic and "slow reading:"

another cornerstone of the curriculum
but also a constraint I'd always suffered from,

having no other choice. Before that, I had only
ever taught poetry

(which had no claim to usefulness, alas—
though it allowed me to give out more As),

and in my current role felt duty-bound
to teach my students everything I wished I'd found

out about at their age: Evidence
must precede argument. Verbs are the heaviest

lifters. Change is constant and inexorable.
The Oxford comma isn't really optional.

You will fall in love. The relationship
will end, though not at the same instant

as the love. Some version of this will continue,
maybe forever, happening to you.

Restate your thesis in the final paragraph.
You can fuck up and still be fine—remember that.

Always include a bibliography.
Don't promise your life to anybody.

★

Now and then, I'd get the strange impression
that *she was me*. A stab of chthonic recognition

would set off a little spasm in my eye.
Sometimes from far away I'd spy

her slanted walk or messy hair and every muscle
in my body would contract. At school,

while my students bent over their exams,
I'd scroll through photos on her Instagram,

the fabric growing damp between my legs
where her finger liked to press

itself inside me like a key. An undiscovered
ancestor. An eidolon. An isomer.

And an uncanny sense of unity,
to love in her what had always seemed deformity

in me. To yield. To feel the snugness of the fit.
To turn the lock. To hear the little click.

★

Cold, ecstatic—walking through the breezeway
to the perfume shop where I was a habitué

that year, which sold fragrances with biomes as their names,
insisting that the body was a place

where events occurred, rather than a thing
to which they happened (to say nothing

of the *cause* of such events)—and buying one
that advertised itself as woodland—"bosky," "sylvan,"

some tree-ish word—and name-dropped Judith Butler on the label,
misting my nape with it and feeling sexual

and unashamed, like a beautiful deciduous slut
of language . . . Oh, I know how ridiculous what

it was I thought in that moment—*I am my own husband*—
but I couldn't stop, I felt that way: bonded

to myself by my authority alone.
No one beside me. No one on the phone.

And going home, writing what I'd seen and heard,
adding detail—deepening the hue—switching a word

to change or nix a sound, feeling my tongue exult
in flights by which experience might vault

beyond the mind, become an externality . . .
Like cells, it's still miraculous to me.

Love found me twice, at once. If it never
happens again I'll still be luckier

than the moon. Breathing, typing these lines,
texting a friend, checking the time,

thinking it wouldn't always be like this,
but still, sometimes, it was.   It is.

★

Then I was the only person in my bed,
though other people's words ran through my head

and kept me company. One was Vivian Gornick,
who demanded: *Put romantic*

love at the center of a novel today,
and who could be persuaded

that in its pursuit the characters are
going to get to something large?

She argued that in modern life
we buy neither the plotline of the happy wife

nor the one where women "self-discover,"
so to speak, by dint of some new lover—

we're too atomized, our institutions too
clearly corrupt. Everything we do

we think we have to do ourselves. But she
was speaking about prose, and the theory

that characters should actualize,
rather than transform as many times

as time allows, as is the case in verse,
where there are barely any characters

at all. In poetry then, let me say that love
has been, above all things, the engine of

self-knowledge in my life—and even after everything
is still what makes the rest worth suffering.

from *n+1*

The Open C

◇   ◇   ◇

You stare into it for days, all your life
as if waiting for a curtain to rise. As if
a production of Ariel and Prospero
were pending in the ocean's void,
the amphitheater of the asteroid.
There's only shocked quartz below.
Where sky and sea are never parted—
there the mass extinction started.

Now resurface, to the serene
compact of our opening scene:
one blue mirror reflects a poreless face,
dazzling evening's investigators.
The other, darker, on the case
shows, in close-up, the craters.

from *Bad Lilies*

The Explanation

◇ ◇ ◇

1.

A boy arrived and took
time to wipe bugs off his windshield;
it was that long ago.

2.

He dragged from his truck
a sack bulging like kidnap;
flakes of meal
spun down the driveway.

3.

It was my turn next. I led him
through deep shade in the grazing
to a spotlit corner
by the bluebell wood.

4.

Everything waited:
mud portholes
rabbits had stupidly left open,
and their game of bowls
abandoned mid-way.

5.

Then: action!
We poured out murder
like water electrified
and a blue charge convulsed the wood.

6.

It was the strangest thing:
dim cries underground,
thumps, and drumming feet
but nothing to see. I took
his hand instead. He would show me.

from *The Hudson Review*

PAUL MULDOON

Joy in Service on Rue Tagore

◊ · ◊ · ◊

1

As I enter a doctor's office
on 57th between Eighth and Ninth
a rat comes zig-zag towards me like a powder-fuse
towards a keg. Every three months

I'd meet Emile in Le Petit Prince
or another high-end restaurant in Algiers.
In Le Normand we bought foie gras by the ounce
even as we rearranged the deckchairs;

it seemed rats given a high dosage of the amaranth
dye found in maraschino cherries
would develop tumors

so he favored mint to garnish his crème de menthe.
Bottoms up, old boy. Cheers.
If he didn't have fresh mint he'd extemporize.

2

If he didn't have fresh mint he'd extemporize
with something from the diplomatic pouch
to simultaneously pep up and put dampers
on our spirits. One woman flashed the badge

of a nipple but looked askance
when I took it in. Once it was all cloak and dagger.
We were all undercover once,
until Emile's headstrong *cri de coeur*

against my using the hand he kept in the fridge
of his apartment on Rue Tagore
to plant a fingerprint on a doorknob chez Ducasse.

In those years it was so much easier to fudge
the evidence, before DNA and my own dodgy ticker,
the years spent chained to a briefcase.

3

The years I spent with a briefcase
chained to my wrist
are as nothing now, those most pervicacious
young creatures I encouraged to do their worst

having long since renounced
their claims or fallen foul of Special Ops.
Every October Emile would make syrup of quince.
He and I have both been toodle-pipped

at the post
by the mediocracy, the closest I now come to a stab
of joy itself being somewhat amorphous—

the fleeting smile, the blood test
proving negative that lends a bounce to my step
as I leave a doctor's office.

from *Raritan*

Haiku Garden

◊   ◊   ◊

Find frogs and toads in
every yard. No garden is
complete without them.

Zipped tight in their sleep-
ing bags—who could imagine
their deep black-eyed dreams?

Piquant peppers please
taunt tease with tongue-piercing taste,
igniting desire.

Of all edible
ovaries, what could taste as
luscious as sweet figs?

Watermelon crossed
Atlantic's perilous waves
with blackseed cargo.

Injuries sustained
while picking berries: snagged skin,
bruised fruit, hurt feelings.

from *Prairie Schooner*

Dame's Rocket

◊   ◊   ◊

Rising straight as canes
around the older farms, the hairy leaves
little arms, the seed for jays,
the fragrance a marriage
of lilac and rose.
They say it came with the early whites
before escaping,
as ornaments may,
the farmyards and gardens
for what's left of the prairie,
congregating sometimes in ditches,
or among century hedgerows,
outliving towns
called Empire and Cicero.

from *The Yale Review*

Fast Track:
Beijing, Montana, Harlem

◇　◇　◇

The Beijing Train Station—my daughter says on Skype—
is a madhouse on a Monday at three a.m.
But I, in the thrall of hawks and antelope,

the closest thing Montana has to mayhem
unless you count the thunder two nights back,
think nothing of it, until, in Harlem,

awake, thanks to an ear-splitting trash truck,
I remember what she said and think again,
unable to conjure up a single flock

of dervish swallows, one sandhill crane
emptying a meadow with its call.
Even the misty valley floor at dawn

seems, from this vantage, hypothetical,
diminished to an image on a screen—
when its abiding genius is its scale.

Is it my failure of imagination
or simply that the human brain can't hold
this much competing information?

fallout from our newly puny world—
Montana giving way to Harlem too fast,
with nothing much to intervene but cloud.

But I also thrill to these absurdly paced—
if not quite majestic—spectacles,
each subway ride an urban vision-quest:

faces, hairdos, fabrics, stiletto heels,
fingers wielding eyeliners and lipsticks
without a smudge to their resplendent nails,

tee-shirts hailing teams or schools or wisecracks
on kick-ass kids who fly in out of nowhere—
the poles makeshift trapezes—nail their tricks,

pass the hat, then move to the next car,
leaving me to translate ads, nostalgic
for *las cucarachas entran pero no pueden salir*

which any passenger from eighties New York
will be able to rattle off forever.
There's even wildlife: rats on the track,

cousins of Montana's muskrat, beaver,
while, above, the newest feral pioneer
is the West's own (a Twitter observer

claims he saw one in a rooftop bar)
supremely adaptable coyote.
Still, no more adaptable than we are,

thirty-eight million of us in a single city,
to get back to my daughter in Beijing
and the dizzying wages of velocity.

But what's diminishing as we're enlarging
our field of vision—what's the toll
(there always is one) we're not acknowledging?

And what's the payoff beyond a jumble
of muddled images we can't quite see
(if we manage to keep hold of them at all)

much less reliably identify?
It's a futile business, accumulation,
thwarted not so much by failing memory

as by a chronic parsimony of attention.
Too late, I realize (I've just turned sixty)
the way I've shortchanged every place I've been;

how a single-minded appetite for novelty
makes every panorama interchangeable,
distinction a finer point of subtlety,

and subtlety, of change so gradual
we're likely to mistake it for duration.
It turns out, I've been insatiable

for precisely the wrong thing. Look at Dickinson,
finite infinity a single room.
Maybe moving around is a distraction,

though I'm not quite sure I can say what from.
My daughter's in China. I'll have to go there.
And another of my daughters lives in Harlem.

But what a pity I never stay longer
in a single spot—any would do,
since, once your gaze begins to linger,

snatches of transcendence glimmer through
even the least welcoming surface;
and there are furtive gems in every view

to which only patience offers access.
That valley in Montana, for example,
always willing, at an instant's notice,

to flaunt its sage, lupine, cattail, thistle,
flash a broadtail hummingbird or two,
throw in, perhaps, a bonus hawk and kestrel

locked in their lopsided pas de deux,
a moose chomping willows in the wetlands . . .
Who knows what grace it's keeping incognito?

Here too (I've moved again; I'm on Greyhound's
Philadelphia Express, a triumvirate
of smokestacks on my left) the Meadowlands

distract me with two herons and an egret
from undetected secrets on my right.
Still, I couldn't say I wholly regret

my rapid-fire pace, however profligate
with unseen wonders. The overstuffed
(from Art Nouveau to Byron to George Eliot)

my go-to habitat—I love a spendthrift,
Bauhaus a chilly afterthought, haiku
for all its nimbleness, a tad bereft

of syllables for my taste, though I do
wish I hadn't missed more than I've seen;
but I'd miss something in every view.

Maybe we all do. Doesn't Dickinson
ignore her—albeit modest—mountain
to focus on its *little gentian*?

Maybe that's the trick: to focus in—
even the miniscule rewards attention—
or better still, to find a way to listen;

everything has truths it could pass on,
each with its own compelling entourage
of likeness and divergence and suggestion

waiting for their instant on a page.
It's too late—sixty!—to indulge them all,
but surely I could hit a higher percentage?

Do I keep moving? or at last stand still?
Either way, it's doubtful I'll find refuge
(is that what I'm after?) from the exile

I'm only just beginning to acknowledge.
But from which Eden? When did I fall?
Or is this what people mean by pilgrimage?

each stop along the way an oblique peephole
onto an interior mirage,
as if all landscape had an inner double,

its buried coordinates always on the verge
of revealing themselves once and for all:
phantom wetlands, alive with plumage;

a dreamscape subway's nonstop spectacle;
a prime, untrammeled swath of acreage
still echoing a sandhill crane's shrill call

through fields of lupine, cattail, thistle, sage
rendered, by a rising mist, invisible
so all you see is space itself writ large
even as what marks it out grows small.

from *Harvard Review*

ROWAN RICARDO PHILLIPS

The First and Final Poem
Is the Sun

◊　◊　◊

The first and final poem is the sun
Which means that poetry is a ritual that the sun organizes and arranges
But, aside from the other, is the singular essential thing
And is one thing among billions upon billions of things just like it
And is known by a name which is not its true name
And so scours, scoured, and will scour the Earth
In search of what it may have been in the beginning and may still be in
　　the end
When time, that invention of the mind, finally reveals
Not the meaning but the meaningfulness of this mystery we call life

from *The Threepenny Review*

Proverbs of Limbo

◇ ◇ ◇

The Buddha is a liquor store
On a busy corner.

The proverbs of Limbo flutter
Between the flames of Righteousness
And the pits of Euphemism.

Gibberish and heredity. Runes
Of light, gnomons of shadow. Bromides
Of *of*.

The Committee on Narrative
Has condemned it, but nevertheless
It may be a lie.

Listen, begins a joke in the form
Of an aphorism, Cancer,
Shmancer—so long as
You have your health.

Listen. The author most quoted
In the Houses of Parliament
Is William Blake. Conviction
Resounds in the byways
Of bloviation. "*Amid*
The lustful fires he walks.
His feet become like brass."

Clashes of theocracies.
The annals of begats and the orders of
Names both balance on the triple pillars
Of Identity of Mystery of Law, all bound
And refuted by the cardboard belt
God wears to amuse the angels.

from *The Threepenny Review*

What's Unsaid

◇   ◇   ◇

How often driving down those roads
we hoped we wouldn't hit something,
the goats we'd passed that morning
herded by that hour so the jackals
wouldn't make quick work of them,
red yolk rupturing over peaks
as we raced the light down the mountain.

Only once did a boar burst out of the woods
like a question just as soon retracted.
Then we were alone again with everything
we didn't say, the wind farms winding
their great arms through nothing,
turning from a place too far to hear.

from *The Atlantic*

Eelam

◇　◇　◇

If my parents were, are, nervy,
camouflaged—against carnivory;

if, at day's end, their choice is
a belief in perpetual crisis;

if this autotomy and playing dead
(a jettisoned tail, ink squirted)

is the only language they
felt it safe to bequeath;

then, to smile today
with unclenched teeth,

to sleep well, not brood—an ingrate—
over trivially frictive grit

till the pearl of nightmare is fished;
to be *at peace*—wouldn't this

betray my parents and my dead,
dismiss as nullity all they did?

from *The American Scholar*

Sentimental Evening

◊ ◊ ◊

The pewter moon's eyebrowed guise
circles a picture of my son. A Windex tear

falls to my son's cheek, and I know
we will never fully know one another.

Message after message asking:
How is the breastfeeding going?

Let me tell you: *Not great. Not great at all.*
Everywhere advice to make the milk come:

plums, fenugreek, blessed thistle.
This morning each stream of water falling

from my showerhead was a knife ready
to gut me. The pewter moon's smile

wants to eat me whole. Online strangers
tell me to love my postpartum body.

They say: You are tiger. You are zebra.
I am desperate to return to the numb feeling

of the surgical theater, the sound
of the doctor mispronouncing my full name.

In the mail a medical bill worth more
than a pickup truck arrives. It arrives before

the state gives my son a social security number,
a birth certificate, a sign of arrival.

Even at my most animal I am the price
of my bearded belly, the price of my crying

breasts, the price of being split,
excavated, vacuumed, and stapled shut.

from *The New Republic*

ROBYN SCHIFF

from Information Desk:
An Epic

◊   ◊   ◊

Contrary to what
         I once believed to be their near-immortal
constitution,
         deprived of oxygen in an old jam jar,
rounded-up body by
         body as they

scrambled under someone's sink
         over the course of
I don't know how many days or weeks
         and brought by coat pocket into
a French Period Room where the Trustees were
         gathered for dinner behind a

folding screen,
         cockroaches landed DOA in proximity
to the writing desk of Louis XV,
         failing thus
to infiltrate that woodwork, itself an
         imitation of Chinese lacquer—

God's plastic—both the secretion
         of the female
Asian scale insect *Laccifer lacca*,
         named for the Sanskrit word for the swarm of
one hundred thousand of her coating a tree
         in a sumptuous

ectoplasm I would like to
        lick,
and a scarlet resin like it—
        thick, deep, sticky, and hard
as the hard candy layer of a candy apple—
        made from the toxic tree sap of a relation

of poison ivy.
        Which is it? Insect or plant?
Who or what? The original black silk velvet blotter
        upon which the King of France unrolled
his map and spread his documented
        mistress was lost

before his giant desk was brought to this
        gallery in the year of my birth.
But matter never disappears
        entirely. I stroke the vestige
of that fabric, chewed up, swallowed,
        metabolized

through the abdomen of silverfish
        and shit-deposited back into earth
where the wild root hairs of an oak tree,
        from which was hewn
this borrowed desk I write this down on,
        groped that desperate

velvet power. *The year of my birth?*
        This very desk?
Endowing me with what self-centered knowledge
        it's my job or fate to disseminate
from the Information Desk? A stranger
        once approached me

there and said,
        "I was on your flight last week!
You were on my plane!"

from *Lit Hub*

Strike Into It Unasked

◇   ◇   ◇

Poetry's "impulse, like electricity, crossing the space, leaves its signature."
—W. S. Graham

No wonder that a flash of sparks
Spills out from what I touch—the LaserJet,

Brimming with static shock,
Suspends invisible electron-clouds

Across the laser-paper's Radiant White
To print "The Windhover"

Electrostatically—
Hopkins's creation-poem, spelled out

In powder-particle black sparks *hard-hurled*
From underlying fire—

The substrate of his poetry
The veiled fire of Christ,

Suffused, incarnate, metaphysical—
And poetry is where

A bird of prey is teetering
Among wind-angles

Intermittently, a fleck
Amid cloud-rhythms, then

A flickering along the morning's
Diamond-edged peripheries,

At such a height, it's there—
Then not—then there again—

Without my realizing it,
Between "The Windhover" and me,

A space is opened, sparking, live,
And I've reached through it, unaware

It *will flame out*, will flare
In a split second of brute force

To jump a gap that's imperceptible
Until I touch the page, and instantly

Hopkins crosses the space
Without a step—

The *wonder of it*, that the briefest touch
Can instigate a shock that's mutual,

As if sheer being, in and of itself,
Is equally as shocked by my existence

As by its own, and equally as startled
To exist as I am here—

Electrons' phantom-loads, drawn off,
Reel back, and hurt me

With a strike as unequivocal
As if it's understood—a law, a truth,

A given—that brute force alone keeps
For itself the power to disclose

The presence of a shining residue
Pent in the fallen world—

Fallen, but even so, *The world is charged*
With power enough to stop the heart—

Electrons, always in the present tense,
Without locality or mass

Or temperature or light—invisible,
Yet capable of spreading in a flash

Across the surfaces of all that is—
Like consciousness lit

For a moment by the thought
That God is worlding, worlding now

And here—even the blearest things,
Objects we overlook, inanimate,

Inert—the sparkling doorknobs,
Shining paper dust, magnetic

Clinging combs, the laser printer's
Thermoplastic case—

Even the blearest things can stun,
Be stunned, are sites

Of inscape-metaphysics where
Materia has taken hold

Of "whatness," "suchness," "isness,"
"Hereness," *laced with fire of stress*—

But even so, such objects only pend
As fragments of a universe

Awaiting a beholder—
Consciousness—

The outbreak of a hidden voltage
Stricken from the ore

Of Hopkins's poetry: titanium,
The paradisal mineral

Whose lightweight metal sheds
The brightest, clearest-selvèd sparks

And most heartstopping firefalls
Before it lets its shining dust

Sheer off, go dark, fall back into itself—
Like humankind—*How fast*

his firedint . . . is gone . . .
In an . . . enormous dark—I stand among

My own footfalls, the imprints of my soles
Mysteriously electrified

And vanishing across the carpet
Where I've *trod* and *trod*, as if my purpose

All along has been to try
To make it visible—the field of force

That hovers over Hopkins's poetry
And brims at margins, boundaries,

White peripheries,
The blinding thresholds where I try

To cross a space as charged and bare
And emptied as the room at 85

St. Stephen's Green, where Hopkins left
His battered shoes behind, because we're meant

To come to God barefoot, and left
The treadmire toil there ("there"

meaning "here") *Footfretted in it*—dust—
And left the footfalls of his poetry

Behind, in disarray,
Scattered, and insufficiently "explained"—

("Novel rhythmic effects," dismissed
By literary interlocutors

As needless, odd, and disagreeable—
A later critic was "repulsed")—

But poetry's *selfbeing* selves itself
Without self-explanation, selves

Without explanatory power,
The way divine creation does—

The way the starry night
Appears—

And Hopkins, as a Greek professor, knew
The ancient word for the divine

Creation is *poiema*—poetry—
And, as a poet, he discerned

Poiema's fire is rapturous and wild
And sudden as a talons-first assault

Out of the blue—Christ's
Striking-in—and knew

That poetry is where a falcon stalls
Midair, prepares to jettison

The cloudbuilt, white
Wingbeaten falcon-footholds

Where contrary winds have brought
The falcon to its highest pitch

Of being—heights upwind
From which to dive headfirst

And upside-down, *hard-hurled*,
With wings pressed shut,

Its livid, bright, *outriding* feet
Drawn back and up,

As if a falcon's feet are useless, weak,
Superfluous impediments

To raptor-plummeting—
Useless, until

The final instant of a strike
So shocking, so unguessed-at, unforeseen,

No prey on earth is able to prepare
For how a nearly imperceptible

And distant hovering
Transforms itself into a

Fraction-of-a-second mortal blow,
The instrike, talons-first, a heralding

Of chaos in the yellow talon-flames
And blackout-wingbeats mantling

The sight of it—the site
Where He consumes the flesh and blood

Of His annihilated prey,
Whose lacerated innocence

He takes into Himself, the way
The *world's wildfire* subsumes

A single flame, to signify
No partial flame exists,

All flames are whole—
As He was first internalized

When He had selved Himself
Into the first and last

Immortal sustenance,
So now His prey is selved

As it becomes a part
Of Him, the Eucharist reversed—

As *in a flash*, a circuit, broken
Violently, is violently restored,

Its suddenness the signal trait
That Jesus emphasized, a sign

The gap is closed between
The kingdom and creation where

God is upstream, and flows
To Christ our Lord—

"Yet I am idle," Hopkins wrote,
Burned out, a socket scorched

Through its interior, without
A visible connection

To its source—useless,
Without effect, like poetry unable

To explain itself, or say
What good it does, or what it's for—

A transcreation of the downstream power
Coursing through what is,

In a creation where all things
Are brimming with a brilliant signature

That will *fall*, *gall*, and *gash*
Itself across the space it opens,

Crossing it—
The way a windhover's

Headlong freefall crazes
The atmosphere with friction-speed

And turns itself into a shining trace—
A blowing-by

As rapturous as if creation
Were an end unto itself

And it's enough that poetry
Strike into it unasked,

And leave a spilling out of sparks
Torn from the *firedint's* continuum

Before the strike—a glimpse
Of the creation, surging past—

from *The Paris Review* and *The Best American Poetry Blog*

Night Visitor

◊   ◊   ◊

I've had more soothing callers at my window:
the muse brushes by like a dangling scarf;
the helium balloon for my neighbor's nuptials,

tied to her guardrail, wafting over my way.
Not him. The window demon comes at night
and jabs at a guitar: the jangling discords

and moonless tones call up the fierce joy
you know only after the burn of sorrow.
He strums the undersides of leaves, roses

the color of blood, silence in the sea's roar.
Hearing those wails, ears that had been dulled
quicken to danger. Mystery. The quieter muse

blows elegies on a muted trumpet.
Swift angels bless the dead and fly away.
But he lands often, toe-heel, and I tremble.

I tremble all the more when he isn't there.

from *The New Republic*

The Hat

◊ ◊ ◊

Aunt Roz lived above her means.
Her one Abyssinian and three Siamese
dined on calves' liver delivered daily
from the fancy butcher, not the A&P.

Her pastel triple-milled French soaps,
packaged like eggs, a dozen to a box—
fragrant tuberose, lily of the valley—
were superior to my mom's plebeian Ivory.

She worshipped culture, dissing her
NJ barbarian sister, my mother, too busy
working in our dress store to groom me
in the arts. Roz got tickets for Price's

Aida and the original *West Side Story*.
She wangled box seats for us to hover
above Arthur Rubinstein's right shoulder.
She got me Maria Tallchief's autograph.

"Artistic" but no artist, Roz lived
la vie bohème, in her rent-controlled
studio apartment a block from NYU,
as if it were a garret in Montparnasse.

Bookkeeper with a high-school GED,
she fancied herself an intellectual.
Exclamation points stabbed the margins
of her Camus's *Stranger* and Paul Valéry.

Raped at thirteen was a story
no one ever talked about. She grew up
gorgeous, had a fling with fledgling
tummler Danny Kaye in the Catskills

hotel-resort her first husband owned.
No one's left to ask about husband No. 2.
Saturdays, she fetched me from ballet
at the Metropolitan Opera House.

We lunched at Lindy's, then bussed
to the bottom of Fifth Avenue.
Holding hands, we skipped through
the streets of Greenwich Village

singing, and everybody smiled at me.
At dusk, Roz unrolled the trundle bed.
She baked fresh popovers for breakfast.
She set up easels, oils, and canvases,

a still-life of pears on her coffee table,
and we painted all Sunday afternoon,
alternating between the styles
of Modigliani and Renoir.

My love for her was unabashed.
My parents tolerated our weekly tryst
but disapproved of Roz's extravagance
while on the dole through family loans.

Unemployed, she gained a hundred pounds
and traded the mind for the body.
Penguins morphed to Harlequins ferried
by the bushel to and from The Strand.

I visited her until I started college.
Prowling Eighth Street for beatnik sandals
and handwrought jewelry, I bypassed
her address. I had aunt fatigue.

She wore me out. She embarrassed me.
I blamed my absences on an allergy to cats,
her cats, who, one by one, succumbed
before Aunt Roz died in a nursing home

when I was forty. Her aqua Le Creusets,
her beat-up ebony coffee table, her flacons
of Cabochard all came to me.
Custom-made dresses from Bendel's.

Her still fabulous costume jewelry.
No one in the family wanted them.
And, just today, I came across her hat
hibernating in its Bonwit Teller box

(itself a collectable, nosegays of violets
floating on white ground) that's been
lost in my closet for some thirty years.
Genuine red fox, *Zhivago*-style, luxurious,

silky, and perfectly preserved,
the crown still stuffed with tissue paper,
must have cost her three weeks' pay.
Purchased, the sweatband's label reads,

in the Oval Room at Ohrbach's—
on 34th Street, the department store
where you'd shop for bargains,
far from Roz's posh uptown salons.

The hat doesn't look half bad on me.
But wearing fur in public is not PC.
Luckily, my nose begins to itch,
my eyes water with unsentimental tears.

Izzy, my gray tabby, sniffs the box.
The crinkled tissue to his liking,
he tamps it down and makes himself at home.
He's not a pedigreed Russian Blue

but a rescue adopted from a shelter,
a pedestrian tomcat, according to Aunt Roz—
snobby, flamboyant, ridiculous Aunt Roz—
a Bonwit's hat in an Ohrbach's box.

from *The New Yorker*

Jack Benny

◊　◊　◊

John Ashbery called me after he died
So you can imagine my excitement
When in his droll hyper-nasalated
Timbre quite undiminished by death
He chatted on about the bowls of
Pitted cherries provided as snack-food
In the upper worlds and of afternoons
Climbing trees with Edna Millay to read
Comic books with her in the branches.
Then his voice dropped two octaves
And he spoke solemnly of Jack Benny:
"You can say funny things or say things
Funny but silence was the punchline
For Jack Benny." And he was gone.

from *The Common*

MAGGIE SMITH

Hope Chest

◇ ◇ ◇

As a bride, given
    away. Then again,

as a wife. Twice taken
    off a man's hands.

As a bride, presented
    as a gift. As a wife,

discarded. Not returned,
    not given back, but

disowned, buck passed.
    Not *doe a deer*

but the kind you pocket
    and spend. Or waste.

My dowry was the dear
    I am, the hope

chest I am, the whole
    of me folded inside

in lieu of linen and lace
    and the good silver,

so now I take it back. Dearly
    I take myself back.

from *The American Poetry Review*

The Bluebird

◊　◊　◊

Each old thing in its new place must prove its worth yet again.
Dust is disturbed, having made itself at home

among what former tenants have found wanting.
A friend brings a gift to brighten my room then leaves

a cruel word to move in with me.
Good and bad don't always line up opposite.

Nearing the end of an earlier journey, I'd stopped at
a roadside motel whose name ameliorated

the experience of staying there
not at all. Around it rose the dark forest of the Shield country,

endless differentiation appearing undifferentiated
though one had the sense of something slowly,

unrelentingly, being taken apart within.
Ahead lay great happiness, great sorrow, and it seems to me now

a decision was to be made between them then,
though the conditions for such a choice did not exist.

The past is so poorly constructed, so unsuited to the living
that must be done, we might wish for the forest to grow up around it—

but knowledge can't replace the facts
of its acquisition. They continue to perform

in the events they set in motion
whether we remember them or not.

I was hungry, it was very late. Across the four lanes
northbound, southbound, divided in my memory

by a waist-high steel girder, a gas station convenience store's
neon still awake. Seldom a break in the traffic,

footbridge miles away. To get to the other side quickly
meant taking your life in your hands.

from *Liberties*

CHRISTOPHER SPAIDE

I'm Not Dying, You're Dying

◊   ◊   ◊

Nothing is so beautiful as Spring—
—Gerard Manley Hopkins

Death is trending so trust me nobody's dreaming.
Bedside, death sits, beaming. Lending some screen time
to the three free minutes of spite spring slings, now streaming.

Daybreaking news—there goes World Insomnia Night.
good morning silent you   March brushes eggwash over
leavened earth, its wish all leaving things might

rise again, sooner rather than never.   *animal*
vegetable or funeral   This year's rebranded earplugs vow
we'll READ IN PEACE, how much? Keeping in minimal

touch, death texts. Sends totals now and again
(again?) of figures snuffed from significance . . .
Ones once, then tens, next thousands, millions when?

click here for the next extinction   Can't pretend
all carnage carves me up the same. I hoard
spare care. But death: I'm asking for a friend.

Three years gone. Three thaws I've seen sun dis-
inter fall's filth, flown nowhere. Three wintry-weepy
autopsy-turvy seasons taught to forecast loss

the moment blossom mobs the magnolias, to start
countdowns like there's no tomorrow.   *there isn't*
Where does our runoff run to? Where's one flooded flowchart

death won't emend to end in death? Can't speak
for our far futures, but in the near I fear
I'll wake and, first thing, before I even pluck

those snug, flush, fleshed, rifled-in slugs from my brain—rip—
bracing for a swelling of swallows, I'll read the news,
what did death do this time.   *time to get up*

from *Bennington Review*

Crown Shyness

◊ ◊ ◊

The ancient epics do not overlap.
Hector dies. Achilles is a ghost.
The wooden horse is backstory at most,
Or hasn't happened yet. A witch's trap
Turns men to swine. A living river burns.
A dog lies pining on a heap of dung.
A woman waits, and is no longer young.
A ransom's paid. A wanderer returns.

So great trees grow, they tell us, putting down
A map of roots that chart the underworld
As deep as topmost leaves reach up, unfurled
Into the blue sublime, and side by side,
Though deep and tall, they only grow so wide,
And hold aloof, not touching at the crown.

*

They hold aloof, not touching at the crown.
Walking between their columns, look above
To see how sky's a river delta of
Blue leaking through, as puzzled light sifts down.
How do they know—how do they sense the touch?
We call it shyness. Is it courtesy,
An antique courtliness of tree to tree,
That somehow knows the border of too much?

When Priam in his laden wagon came
Under the veil of night to meet his foe,
And buy the body of his son, laid low,
Achilles drew back from his savage brink
To courtesy, and said, "We are the same:
Though princes, we are mortals. Eat. Drink."

★

"Though princes, we are mortals. Eat. Drink."
So all that bloodshed ends, in a shared feast,
Stories, tears. Dawn kindles in the East,
The westering stars go ashen as they sink.
As neutral birds erupt in morning choirs,
Mules shake their ears, their hides atwitch with flies.
There's nothing for the living but to rise
And to prepare the wood for funeral pyres.

The forest groans and braces for the axe:
So many trees it takes to burn a man!
Nine days they gather wood from every side.
Between the trees, there open up dirt tracks
For mules and sledges. Now the thwacks elide
In rhythms that no bard has ever scanned.

★

In rhythms that no bard has ever scanned,
The timber falls. It's timber when it falls
And crashes into silence with its calls
Of birdsong and its rustling sarabande,
A library of turning leaves; its rings
A record of the years no needle traces,
Shade the annihilating sun erases,
Torn from the catalogue of living things.

(It started with the catalogue of ships:
Whole forests felled for keels, masts, spars, oars, hulls
Made black and waterproof with tar and pitch.
The sight of the armada stirred the pulse
Of men more than the hair, the skin, the lips
Of beauty's queen men later called a bitch.)

★

The beauty queen men later called a bitch
(She called herself that sometimes) stood aloft
Upon the ramparts, while the old men coughed
And young men died, and thought how it was rich—
No wedding could go off without a hitch!—
Men blamed her for their bloody-minded slaughter.
She missed her ex sometimes. She missed her daughter.
She'd go to Egypt, and become a witch.

There near the wall a fig tree grew. Its shade
In summer made the city street a park
Where all the little Trojan children played,
Chasing each other round the wall, all games
Until their mothers called as it grew dark
And they became a litany of names.

★

The shades become a litany of names.
They creep up to the trough of blood to drink.
And now the fog clears—they can speak and think.
His mother nears to say she never blames
Him for her death of—here her sigh is sharp—
A mother's broken heart. His father, well,
He lives in squalor, half a man, a shell.
His wife—she plays those "suitors" like a harp.

(Someday he'll show his father as he grieves
The orchards he was promised: thirteen pears,
Ten apple trees, two scores of figs, and vines
That make the best homebrew a vineyard bears,
Not strong as Agamemnon's sea-dark wines,
But sweet and bright, like light through olive leaves.)

★

Sweet and bright, like light through olive leaves
The dawning of his homecoming. Yet still
She doesn't recognize him. But she will!
Unless it is deception that she weaves?
Has someone moved the marriage bed? "What brute. . . !"
He starts to say. And then he sees she smiles,
And knows they are well wedded in their wiles,
Bed carved from one tree, anchored at the root.

In sleep, though, king and queen are like two oaks,
Grown deep and tall, and yet not touching quite.
One dreams of battle, one of breaking yolks;
One hears house sparrows, one the rhythmic slap
Of oars; one ravels, one swims waves all night.
Their ancient epics do not overlap.

from *The Sewanee Review*

Wallace Stevens Comes Back to Read His Poems at the 92nd Street Y

◊   ◊   ◊

It was a willfulness, an exertion, which verged
At once on fluency, that I should appear, as I did
Today, out of light-blue air, in a dark-blue suit.

In the time that I have been gone, I never outgrew
The sensation of being, nor for a moment forgot
Which world was mine. I clung to the merest whispers,

The faintest echoes that rose from below. For years,
I lay on a down-filled sofa, alone with my passions.
Bright refrains of endless azure circled

The hours, and filled me with pleasure, but the poems
I wrote were dulled by the sort of calm one feels
In the downward drift of sleep. They never became

The relics of light I wished them to be. In the days
When it could be said I was one of you, I loved
The beyond as somebody only can who is bound

By the earth. All that I wrote was a hymn to desire,
To the semblances and stages of bliss. My poems
Bore only a passing likeness to the life

Of which they were the miraculous part. But when
I was borne among the erasures of heaven I began
To believe that whatever was distant or puzzling could never

Be made too obvious. Of course I was wrong.
I'd allowed myself to be swayed by a vision of plainness
That would have all things turn into one idea.

So much for the past. May the worst of it fall by the wayside
Tonight. May other more intricate powers convene.
May the words that I speak be the ones you hear.

from *The New Yorker*

The Days

◊   ◊   ◊

If only I could live my life, not write it,
I'd have double the experience

and be better at nothingness, at being present.
The page, I once believed, offers permanence,

sanctifying time, making it longer,
but now I see my words as susceptible,

even if digital, to fire, flood, misplacement.
To misinterpretation. To accidental

download by enemy. I don't yet want them
to be lost, but I dread the possibility

that they won't self-destruct at the end
of my life, or the end of my lucidity.

Maybe I've been using paper all wrong,
committing to ink what should live in my head,

which is part of my body, which will not last.
Long ago, in college, a friend once said

he would never keep a journal; he preferred
to live in the moment. Back home in June,

I threw the lot of them, dating back to childhood,
into a rose-red shopping bag—we reused

every one—then put the bag out with the trash.
Thank the stars or our thrift for its luminosity:

my mother asked what was in it, then ran
down the driveway, hauled it back up. Her family

had once lost everything. She knew what I wanted
to be, what I already was. "You have to keep them!"

she yelled. She never yelled. Even my friend,
hearing it later, said the same. What worked for him

might not be right for me. He loved to argue
and was always there, vociferous, ready to engage,

while I was too receptive, too easily swayed,
though I often swatted back. That's what college

is for, the wisdom goes, late-night conversation
with challenging peers. A few years later,

we were no longer friends, not through conflict
but cliché: he had wanted more, I had demurred,

and then there was nothing to say. But maybe
I'd been partial to aspects of his attention—

maybe all the platitudes were true. I had failed
to consider, despite constant reflection,

what my being there must have conveyed.
Reflection is simply an image, a face in a mirror;

to look upon is not the same as to examine.
Perhaps there is such a thing as a neutral observer.

Each night I had written *Here is what happened*
like a kid whose pen makes her small life exciting,

then gone on mistaking the plot for the story,
as if the point of writing were writing.

from *The New Yorker*

Pe'ahi Light

◇   ◇   ◇

1

Half-filled with sand, a Karatsu tea bowl
placed on a writing desk: no incense

smokes the air; above, on a wall, *heart*,
brushed in three strokes, where the black

ends of each stroke flare into the void.
We zigzagged across a dry streambed;

that night, a breeze surged like incoming surf—
waves of rain crashed, subsided, plunged;

now, in Pe'ahi light, rain patters the fronds,
glistens the fishtail palms, the stilt root palms,

the white elephant palm, butterfly palm,
a palm, twenty inches tall, risen out

of a split coconut. *Drizzle, rain, downpour—*
I have no words for these kinds of rain;

I mark a conch shell doorstop, a dictionary
of etymology: *rain*, from Old English,

regn—a frond emerges out of the dark—
rain stops, water beads at the tips of ferns.

2

Geckos click and squiggle up a windowpane;
crisscrossing palm fronds and blades

of sunlight block lines of sight; when a frond
sways, you sway, tingling in yellow light,

arched forty feet above ground; when
a frond stills, you still, mark a spray of red ginger.

On another continent, a man lies strapped
to a hospital bed and can't rampage

across a room he no longer recognizes.
Before opening a window, you pause

at desiccated geckos caught between a screen
and windowpane. Are we ensnared

by hazards we cannot comprehend?
A feral chicken clucks below the house.

You spy a Tahitian lime on a branch, another
yellowing farther up. On a far shore,

two women shriek as one reels in a silver
fish that bounces along the surface of lake water.

3

Sitting on a round blue cushion in a room
with three white walls, where a fourth

has screened glass doors that open
onto a lanai, I focus on the spackled

ceiling and, finding contours of mesas
and arroyos from the air, know I overlay

these shapes onto emptiness. As warm air
flows in, I smell clusters of white ginger

flowering below; earlier, we walked
a trail down a bluff to where Papalua Stream

empties into Pilale Bay and saw divers
out among white-capping waves. Did they

dive for reef triggerfish? Octopi? In the space
of not-knowing, I ~~float~~ joy when

the ~~body~~ mind unfolds and ~~tolls~~ flowers
from inside the ~~bell~~ gong of silence,

and I spark when ~~language~~ love—~~1457~~,
~~sudden unexpected attack or capture~~—surprises.

4

Facing east, blue lions flank the front door—
a machete, hat, compass, splintered

ukulele mounted on a wall quiet
this room; on a desk, a globe maps

the world known to Europeans in 1745;
today we can map the fractal

contours of a coastline, but what's
never obsolete is the unappeasable urge

to speak. A couple hikes a switchback
trail down to the bay; sitting in the shade,

we overhear, "*Fuck* this, *fuck* that,"
some stomping, then they disappear.

An impoverishment of language's
an impoverishment of life; we want

to see the empty sky fly into pieces,
to incorporate three systoles

in writing *heart* and bloom
through lifetimes within a single lifetime.

5

Carols an 'amakihi in the forest after a shower—
the pendant lobster claws of a heliconia

gleam in sunlight amid a green thicket of leaves.
This morning we bobbed in ocean waves,

swam in sight of an island with a single palm
at the summit, observed flat-bottomed,

cumulus-topped, steel-blue clouds sail
low over water, listened to surf break

over black lava rock, over black lava rock;
scanning the horizon's curving rim,

I yearned to see a pod of humpback whales,
but, through binoculars, saw an endless

shimmer of wave crests that stung my eyes.
Now, as a gecko darts across eucalyptus flooring,

as I strive to make a poem that scintillates
in the dark, scintillates in the dark,

we do not stagger, zombie zapped,
but spark in our bodies glistening in misting rain.

from *Poetry*

The Field Is Hot and Hotter

◊ ◊ ◊

To float on something she has never seen,
my daughter will need her teeth, which she did
not get from me. Her liver, yes. Her death
also. Her breath, no. To float, she will not
need to be lighter than air, just lighter
than terror, whose volume increases with
heat. She will not need her peach cheeks. The green
of her eyes neither. Terror is a color
-less field. I gave her the nails she will need,
and the hammering feet. The field is hot
and hotter. This is a matter of speed.
A question of how much. A question of
weather. The question is whether the seed
will live. It is not a question of love.

from *TriQuarterly*

A New Year

◇ ◇ ◇

Was it myself I left behind? Or was
the country letting go of itself at each clackety-clack
as the train rattled northward into dusk?
Girders flashed by, the ghosts of factories.
Then frozen fields, their stubble narrowly laid out
in an ancient, foreign, indecipherable script.
New solitudes flared on the smutty pane.
As if I were aging faster than the engine's hurtle . . .
While the Hudson shoved its massive, wrinkled drowse
south, dreaming at its own pace: the drowned
river, carrying thousands of years
of sediment through torn uterus of rock.
Angry signs slashed the shadows. Wrecked cars
stacked in yards, tilting fences, sheds
pledged revenge. Then a whoosh of snow
tattered the trees and night swallowed us whole.

Till dawn, jerking me from my berth,
broke over Indiana's frost-bitten furrows,
a country graveyard slotted among farms.

from *The New Yorker*

Ashkenazi Birthmark

◊   ◊   ◊

Maybe the parapsychologists are right
To claim that birthmarks
Intimate wounds sustained in prior lives,

An idea darker & more complex than believing
The heart-shaped stain on your daughter's back
Resulted from a mother's love of strawberries.

This perfectly round benign brown button
Sewn onto my forehead in the womb
Must speak of a maternal great-uncle

Executed in Vinnytsia, 1942,
The bullet hole from which a plume of smoke
Escaped like a soul, if one believes in souls . . .

That whole side of the family gone now,
No one to ask about the ancestor
Named Alexei or Grigory or Ze'ev

Whose corpse bore a bullet hole on his brow,
This birthmark through which the unhoused wisp
Spirals into cursive to strike this page.

from *The Gettysburg Review*

from The Life of Tu Fu

◇   ◇   ◇

I eat in the rain, under the river willows.

I lean on the railing.

I write poems about what I see, for things pass so quickly.

This morning the clouds are thin.
Last night the moon was yellow.

★

Peach blossoms in the river current; ducks below the dock.
A single seagull, tossed around in the wind.

It is beneath you never to forget petty slights.

★

When birds call they call to their own kind.
Gibbons hang from the branches and imitate each other.
Gulls stand in a line side by side and think only of themselves.

Thirty years since I've seen you and I still see you getting on the boat.
Ashes smolder in a heart that's died.

★

They sell their children to pay the taxes.
They hope their counterfeit coins will work.

The army has taken all the horses;
even the officials ride mangy donkeys.

Today is like yesterday.
Troops still on the Central Plain.

They say that when a goose flies south it holds a twig in its beak to
keep from making a sound the hunters might hear.

★

The body grows weaker, but gazing at the mountains remains the same.
In the distance, smoke rises from the scattered houses burned by
marauders.

Their pennants are the tails of black horses.
Their swords are forged with patterns of stars.

Is there anyone left, under a leaking roof, looking out the door?
They even killed the chickens and the dogs.

★

A white horse with two arrows in its empty saddle.

The corpses lying by the road change so much in a single day.

I wish I could talk with someone.

★

The only people I meet are people I've never known.

I thought of Chuang Tzu: "Be careful not to disturb the human mind."

You'll weep for reasons other than the war.

There's a lot to see on a dead-end road,
but not much kindness.

Bitter bamboo so bitter
insects won't eat it.

Bitter bamboo so low
birds won't nest in it.

Bitter bamboo so weak
it's useless for building.

Bitter bamboo to plant around my hut.

Today I am not happy.
The heart is not a stone that can be rolled.

★

They say that rocks turn into swallows in the rain, and back to rocks
when it clears.

They say that when it rains for seven days, a leopard does not hunt,
and cultivates the patterns in its coat.

They say there is a certain thunderclap when a carp turns into a
dragon.

They say that a chicken has five virtues: civil talents, military talents,
courage, moral rectitude, and fidelity.

They say that when a master archer shoots, his prey drops at the twang
of the bowstring.

No one understood when I wrote "The sun rises from its bath like a
duckweed."

The sea accepts the water from all the streams.

★

The war goes on: I live among deer.
I sit out in the moonlight and moonlight shines on my knees.
I sit out even when it rains.

I thought of the sage Wang Hui-chih who was appointed to the
Ministry of Mounts. Asked what his duties were, he said he did not
know, but people were always bringing him horses. Asked how many
horses, he said a sage doesn't think about horses.

from *The Paris Review*

The Man with
the Yellow Balloon

◇ ◇ ◇

Did you ever see the man with the yellow balloon?
He used to walk around Lower Manhattan,
mostly with his head down, brow
quizzically grooved, usually in crowds.
I first saw him outside Port Authority in 2002.
Across 8th Ave, I saw the yellow balloon.
It bobbed like a bee above one tall flower.
I told Jeff, and he didn't believe me,
but then Jeff and I saw him in the East Village,
E. 5th between Aves A and B;
we saw the whole dude that day;
he was wearing a khaki trench,
carrying a briefcase, minding his business.
A tallish guy, white, bald, maybe fifty.
From his head floated a yellow balloon.
It was fat with helium. A few inches of twine
and a blue-and-orange headband
kept it from floating away. This alone
—a yellow balloon leashed to a Mets or Knicks
colored headband—would have been enough
never to forget, but that wasn't even all.
There was a scrap of foil taped or glued
around the yellow balloon's nozzle.
The guy had pinched up threads
so the foil looked screwable.
It was a fricking comic strip light bulb.
Dude was just walking along E. 5th like that!

The rubber light bulb jittered and jerked in the wind,
shaking a yellow mood into the twilight.
I christened him "The Man with the Yellow Balloon."
Jeff dubbed him "Dr. Light Bulb."
We sat, as we did in 2002, at Sophie's, a bar,
drinking $2 cans of Pabst.
Jeff had been in New York four years,
but I was a year older; his big idea
was that Dr. Light Bulb was a piece
of one-man performance art
invented by Dr. Light Bulb himself, a unique soul
who lived with his mother in Queens.
Or Dr. Light Bulb had a street-level job
advertising tax services or a comedy club;
he stood on a corner for hours on end
emitting a yellow beep of visual noise,
and his briefcase was full of pink and green fliers
that no human being has ever wanted.
He'd just finished his shift and now was like
a waiter walking home still in a necktie.
"Not bad," I said. "Not bad." I tilted my head
at a 22-year-old slant, and sucked on my cigarette,
a recent addition to my poet costume.
No, the man with the yellow balloon
was neither of those: he was loftier by far.
He was a twisted, silly, Gatsbian son of God.
His freaky idea hovered above him like a yellow womb
and a whole person came out of it,
born into the street's eyes ceaselessly.
The man sowed a merry confusion,
and the memories of the yellow balloon-bulb
he spread among city-dwellers were like apple seeds.
"Yep," I said, "plus you also got the whole
'tongues of fire' thing." I stared up into the smoke
that clings to tin ceilings above 22-year-old poets.
I liked the yellow balloon better than Jeff.
Perhaps I liked it better than anyone.
When you're newly in love with someone
you like near everything about them,
and I was so in love with New York City

that I even liked it when it scared me.
I liked the hot rank air that subway entrances
exhaled on summer mornings. I liked its pigeons
on the iron zigzag of every fire escape,
and I loved the thousands of strangers' faces,
that throbbing bobbing tide of faces
and the sensation of having such a face
that appears and is gone. I paused, back then,
for any act of break dancing.
Like these things, the yellow balloon-bulb
struck me hard as a New York thing;
it had sprung, ghostly as a mushroom,
out of the city's anonymity,
out of the namelessness of anyone's face.
Anyway, after that night with Jeff
I carried the balloon around, front of my brain,
like a tiny flame in a pan. It amazed me.
I was amazed it was even intelligible.
A 20th century symbol of sudden knowledge
(light → Edison's light bulb → comic strip → speech),
and here it was, worn out into the city
as a foil-nozzled yellow balloon.
Somehow it was not only possible, but real.
Anyway, I started looking out for it.
Biking to my new job, in a joy of wind, trout leaping
in my thighs (on account of some poem in my head),
I threaded Jeff's yellow hand-me-down Peugeot
west on Houston through a traffic of cabs,
and at red lights, I looked for a blip of yellow.
I looked for it above the masses of heads,
a jittering thing, sensitive to the wind as a licked thumb.
I looked for it up the avenues, bopping others.
It was ok if I didn't get to see it.
Other people, I thought, were getting to see it.
And I'd imagine them having seen it,
and it flashing upon their inward eyes
before they slept, the sort of bright dot
a city day can disappear around.
I also asked the people I talked to if they'd seen him,

if they'd seen the man with the yellow balloon.
I asked Jack the comedian. He said he had.
Down on Delancey by the Happiness Deli.
What was he doing? "Buying your mom a sandwich,"
said Jack. Jack had gotten an apartment
with Toby the Sex Addict, a hulking blond farm boy
who'd played minor league hockey
and now taught skating lessons in Chelsea.
Jack had been in a month-to-month deal,
one of those plywood-room-in-an-industrial-space
situations that used to be what you thought of
when someone said he lived in Williamsburg.
That was how he met Toby, who was 25,
which seemed old to us. Toby was trying
to discover himself as a painter,
but the only paintings we ever saw him do
were watercolors of unsuspecting women
at the bar on Ludlow that used to be the piano store.
Toby's brother was a manager; that's how Toby got in.
We got in to keep an eye on Toby.
He would set up shop at a corner table,
and Jack and I would giggle like schoolchildren
watching as he walked up to women, ages 21–60,
holding his hideous portraits: "It's you."
And yet he always found a taker.
Furious coupling noises plagued Jack's every dawn.
He wore bags under his eyes.
Anyway, Toby thought the yellow balloon
sounded "beautiful," even if he hadn't seen it,
and for a night he added it to the air
above the heads of his smeared women.
And I have no idea why I include any of that,
but it was New York; it was the fall of 2002.
I asked Mal the boy genius poet
if he'd seen the yellow balloon; he was twenty
and lived across town with a mouthful of cavities
and a gorgeous collection of cigarette butts
a wheezing printer and papers everywhere in a crumbling
second-story cave above a bar.

Mal hadn't seen him but was intrigued;
"Was the man wearing sunglasses?"
When I said he wasn't, Mal was impressed. Brave!
How many times, one wonders, were calls
of "Eh Einstein, what's the big idea?"
or "Eh buddy got any bright ideas?"
lobbed in his direction? Daily, it had to be daily.
And did he go out into the world daily?
Weekly? With Mal it dawned on me
that the balloon wasn't the same balloon (a soft explosion
that should have happened earlier).
It had to be a new balloon each day.
It was the same headband, in all likelihood,
but it was a fresh yellow balloon, a new string.
Did he own a helium tank? Was it the same scrap of foil?
(Maybe he had a ball of foil and peeled,
each day, a scrap of foil off it, and wrapped
the fresh hope of a new balloon?)
My explanations grew only more elaborate.
There would come a point each day
where each yellow balloon would pucker
inward like a dying pear. After a day
of being buffeted, each balloon would droop.
What's sadder than a sagging balloon?
Towed along, it would broadcast that a man
had an idea that hadn't panned out.
Or maybe the man never let it get to that.
Maybe he cut the string, and with his hand visoring his eyes,
watched his yellow balloons, like released fish,
one at a time, rise between buildings.
I wanted to find the man and talk to him.
I wanted to know who he was and why.
I told all this to Jade the playwright
(she wasn't yet Jade the dead novelist)
in her darkened first-floor bedroom/office/living room/kitchen;
she wrinkled the corners of her eyes
sucked her Camel, loosed a cumulus.
"No you don't," she said. "That dude's the last dude
you EVER want to have a conversation with."

How'd she know? Because she'd seen him around,
thought he might be useful, like, in a play,
like he or someone like him might walk by or something,
be a topic of conversation or something.
So she'd asked Ellen about him; Ellen was 33.
She'd bartended at Mars Bar, amazingly,
since she was 20; the whole Lower East Side
had an active crush on her. Jeff did; Jack did;
I would have had one had they not beat me to it.
Anyway, Ellen was an expert in the whack-jobs
from Bowery east to Ave D.
They were already, in 2002, dwindling in number.
Apparently the man has been, off and on,
walking around in a yellow balloon for over a decade.
And for over a decade, when asked,
he's had basically the same reply.
He claims he's looking for his next big idea.
He has a logic: in the way it's easier to do something
once you've lied and said you've already done it
by ambulating in a foil-nozzled yellow balloon
"the light bulb is able to come on."
He says this all with a straight face, a stern
Eastern European sort of mien, then smiles.
He's an artist, he says, and an ethno-sociologist
and a professor of (the destruction of)
metaphysics. He dabbles in film photography. He has
a card. And money, surprisingly. He talks offhandedly
about his gallerist; his gallerist this, his gallerist that;
he doesn't have a gallerist. He has a seat
at the bar at Max Fish, and his yellow balloon
wiggles under the ceiling fan. He waits.
In time, he finds takers, doe-eyed whimsical types,
drunk, with hair dyed silver or pink,
who love the idea of acting like transfixed
two-year-olds at the sight of a damn balloon.
Ellen got it from Norman who got it from
Old Steve the Oracle that the Yellow Balloon Man
squatted his way into a deed on Ave C.
This was back in the '80s. He sold big in the late '90s.

Now he takes the train in from Jersey.
He fashions himself as . . . hmmm . . . a success.
More than that. He situates himself as a master,
spin-doctors the cracks in his face by reference
to Warhol's Factory, as if he was there.
Maybe he was. Who cares. His yellow balloon
ain't art. It's the farthest thing from it.
It doesn't have allure. It IS a lure. There's a difference.

from *New York Quarterly*

KEVIN YOUNG

Diptych

◇   ◇   ◇

NIGHT WATCH

You can fall in love
in a museum, but only

with the art
or its silence—or the stranger

you don't mean to follow

suffering past the Old Masters
& the unnamed

servants. Rembrandt's face
half in shadow—

you can fall for what
isn't there already, or

with the 13th century—the swan
raising up, roosters hung

upside down to die on a cross—

Even the tourists gathered
round the docent, the same

jokes & half-truths,
loom beautiful—

the children crying hurried
out of sight. Forget

The Night Watch, the crowds,
instead follow the quiet

to the portraits of light
entering a room. These walls,

few windows, hold
the world—what the world

couldn't say till someone
saw it first—and now

it's everywhere. The braids
  of that woman's hair.

SELF-PORTRAIT WITH FELT HAT

One should never be in love

when in a museum—
  better to be alone, if not
utterly, then practically—

tired of feet, & routine,
  forge ahead beyond
the bounds of audio-tours

& family, isolate, avoid
  this couple oblivious
to it all, the captions & arrows,

kissing like no tomorrow
  beside Van Gogh's sunflowers—
bruised, chartreuse, brilliant

& wilting for years, yet never
  managing to. Skip
holding hands & Gauguin's

portrait of Van Gogh
  painting what he saw. The crows
gather like clouds, black—

or the crowds—that the couple
  doesn't care about—
numb to all else. Best

  believe in the world
more than yourself.

from *Poetry*

CONTRIBUTORS' NOTES AND COMMENTS

KIM ADDONIZIO was born in Washington, D.C., in 1954. Her recent poetry collection is *Now We're Getting Somewhere* (W. W. Norton, 2021). She is the author of seven other poetry collections, two novels, two story collections, and two books on writing poetry, *The Poet's Companion* (with Dorianne Laux; Norton, 1997) and *Ordinary Genius* (Norton, 2009). Her memoir, *Bukowski in a Sundress: Confessions from a Writing Life*, appeared from Penguin Books in 2016. *Exit Opera* is due in September 2024. She lives in Oakland, California, and teaches poetry workshops on Zoom.

Of "Existential Elegy," Addonizio writes: "I have twenty-odd pages of drafts and notes for this piece. I'd given my students a writing prompt: find an interesting quotation and respond to the idea(s) in it. I'm always trying to think of ways to move them—and myself—beyond the anecdotal and into the multivalent, mysterious place where poetry lives. Browsing quotations from existentialist philosophers led me to de Beauvoir and Sartre. I reordered several lines, deep-sixed many sentimental statements about my cat, and struggled, as I often do, to figure out an ending. I thought about D. A. Powell's concept of elegies that refuse consolation, which is how the image highlighting de Beauvoir's grief at the loss of her longtime partner/lover/fellow philosopher migrated to the final line. Another of her quotes that spoke to me: 'Life is occupied in both perpetuating itself and in surpassing itself; if all it does is maintain itself, then living is only not dying.' I like the idea that poetry, too, perpetuates and surpasses itself and our existence."

HOWARD ALTMANN's *Forgive Time*, an original collection of fifty poems, was translated into Hebrew by award-winning poet/translator, Tal Nitzán, and was published by Keshev Press (Czesław Miłosz,

Wisława Szymborska, Tomas Tranströmer) in 2021. Born and raised in Montreal, Canada, Altmann lives in New York City.

JULIA ALVAREZ has been practicing the craft of writing for more than fifty years. Her books include the novels *How the García Girls Lost Their Accents, In the Time of the Butterflies*, and *Afterlife*; books for younger readers; collections of poetry, including *Homecoming, The Other Side*, and *The Woman I Kept to Myself*; and nonfiction. Her latest novel is *The Cemetery of Untold Stories*, and she is currently assembling a collection of poems to be called *Visitations*. Alvarez is one of the founders of Border of Lights, a movement to promote peace and collaboration between Haiti and the Dominican Republic. She lives in Vermont.

Of "Amenorrhea," Alvarez writes: "As a female, growing up in the 1950s in a Latina family, I was taught that my primary goal in life was to become a mother and thereby help to create the next generation. Once we emigrated for the States, my dream changed: I wanted to become a poet (my first true love). But even here in liberated USA, I encountered the same subtle assumptions. One of my college professors pronounced that for a woman to decide not to have a child was to commit 'genetic suicide.' (Thank you very much, Patriarchy!) When in my late thirties, my menses stopped, the biological rug was pulled out from under me. Plan B was not to be. All I had left to contribute to a future generation was my writing, and what if that failed, too? The poem centers on that existential fear. Zero at the bone. The line stops here."

CATHERINE BARNETT teaches in NYU's MFA Program in Creative Writing and works as an independent editor. Her most recent collection of poetry is *Solutions for the Problem of Bodies in Space* (Graywolf Press, 2024). Her three other collections are *Human Hours* (*The Believer* Book Award in Poetry), *The Game of Boxes* (James Laughlin Award of the Academy of American Poets), and *Into Perfect Spheres Such Holes Are Pierced* (Beatrice Hawley Award). A Guggenheim Fellow, she received a 2022 Award in Literature from the American Academy of Arts and Letters.

Of "Apophasis at the All-Night Rite Aid," Barnett writes: "When my son was little, I craved the brightly lit solitude of a mostly unoccupied midnight drugstore: the order, the possibilities, the suggestion of cures for problems I hadn't known had either already happened, or would soon happen. What can't a new sample size of Eucerin resolve?

Almonds on half-price sale. There used to be two drugstores one block from my apartment, but they've been replaced by a Krispy Kreme and a dollar store, which are also temptations, if of a different sort. The moon is an antidote for many things and can, if you're so inclined, send a little shot of dopamine straight into your disbelieving mind. So is a handsome pharmacist, who wouldn't really be found at the actual store at that hour but is the perfect imaginary companion."

JOSHUA BENNETT is a professor of literature at MIT. He is the author of five books of poetry, criticism, and narrative nonfiction. *Spoken Word: A Cultural History* (Knopf, 2023) was named one of *The New York Times*'s 100 Notable Books of 2023. *The Study of Human Life* (Penguin, 2022) won the Paterson Poetry Prize, and is being adapted for television in collaboration with Warner Brothers Studios. Born in New York City in 1988, he lives in Massachusetts with his family.

Bennett writes: "I wrote 'First Philosophy' a year or so after my wife and I moved into our home, and our son had just started walking, running, yelling throughout the house. It was my attempt, I think, to express both a certain kind of gratitude, and a sense of everyday astonishment that I hadn't felt in a long time. I started seeing miracles all around me, and I wanted to get some of that experience down on paper."

Born in Massachusetts in 1956, APRIL BERNARD is the author of six books of poetry—most recently, *The World Behind the World* (Norton, 2023)—as well as two novels and numerous essays. She lives in Saratoga Springs, New York, and teaches at Skidmore College.

Of "'Sithens in a net,'" Bernard writes: "'Sithens' is an archaic, tongue-twisting form of the word 'since.' Certain phrases (from Wyatt and other poets of the sixteenth century) stick in my head; recently a raft of poems arrived, in direct and indirect response to their words. This is one of them."

CHRISTOPHER CHILDERS was born in Memphis, Tennessee, in 1982 and lives in Baltimore, Maryland, where he teaches Latin, coaches squash, and benevolently regards his pet fish and budgies. *The Penguin Book of Greek and Latin Lyric Verse*, entirely translated by Childers, was published by Penguin Classics in 2024.

Childers writes: "A μίασμα in Greek refers to a 'stain, defilement, or pollution' an individual or community has incurred as a result of harboring, wittingly or not, some monstrous guilt. A sort of spiritual smog, it emanates from the soul of a single person but tends to result in nonspiritual collective punishment, such as fire or plague. My poem 'Miasma' was written pretty early during the 2020 lockdowns and then forgotten about until I stumbled on it in a file last summer and started submitting, never imagining it would end up in *BAP*! While I certainly don't believe that the COVID-19 pandemic was caused by a modern-day Oedipus or Coronis, I do feel that the whole experience shrank many souls, including my own, making us smaller and meaner, and that the consequent spiritual malaise could not have been good for the public health."

AMA CODJOE was born in Austin, Texas, in 1979 and raised in Youngstown, Ohio. Her *Bluest Nude* (Milkweed Editions, 2022) won the Lenore Marshall Poetry Prize. She has received fellowships from the Rona Jaffe Foundation, the National Endowment for the Arts, the Bronx Council on the Arts, the New York State Council/New York Foundation of the Arts, and the Jerome Foundation. Codjoe was the 2023 Poet-in-Residence at the Guggenheim Museum. She is the winner of a 2023 Whiting Award.

HENRI COLE was born in Fukuoka, Japan, in 1956 to a French mother and an American father. He has published twelve collections of poetry, most recently *Gravity and Center: Selected Sonnets, 1994–2022* (Farrar, Straus and Giroux, 2023). He has received many awards for his work, including the Jackson Prize, the Kingsley Tufts Poetry Award, the Rome Prize, the Berlin Prize, the Lenore Marshall Award, and the Medal in Poetry from the American Academy of Arts and Letters. He is also the author of *Orphic Paris* (New York Review Books, 2018), a memoir. He teaches at Claremont McKenna College.

Of "At Sixty-Five," Cole writes: "This poem was inspired by Hans Magnus Enzensberger's poem 'At Thirty-three.' He was a marvelous German poet who lived to be ninety-three."

BILLY COLLINS was born in the French Hospital in New York City in 1941. He was an undergraduate at Holy Cross College and received his PhD from the University of California, Riverside. His books of poetry include *Musical Tables* (Random House, 2022) and *Aimless Love: New and Selected Poems* (Random House, 2013). He is a former Distinguished Professor of English at Lehman College (City University of New York). A frequent contributor and former guest editor of *The Best American Poetry* series, he was appointed United States Poet Laureate 2001–2003 and served as New York State Poet 2004–2006. He also edited *Bright Wings: An Illustrated Anthology of Poems about Birds*, illustrated by David Sibley (Columbia University Press, 2010). He was recently inducted into the American Academy of Arts and Letters.

Of "The Monet Conundrum," Collins writes: "This little hinge poem revisits a question known to haunt creative people of all stripes, in this case, a poet: is each poem one writes a distinct work of art, or are all the poems really the same poem just dressed up in different words? Somehow, the question brought to mind Monet's series of paintings, *Haystacks*. Each one of the twenty-five he produced in one year is certainly different, mostly due to variations in light, weather, and the season. A few are even topped with fresh snow. But they all look like, well . . . haystacks. These obsessive plein air paintings of one common object, done near his home in Giverny, seemed like a possible way to illustrate that burning question. The disappointing answer, by the way, must be both. It all depends on whether you are looking at the duck or the rabbit—the similarities or the differences—to borrow a pet image from Wittgenstein."

BRENDAN CONSTANTINE was born in Los Angeles, California, in 1967. He teaches at the Windward School, and, since 2017, has been developing workshops for writers living with aphasia and traumatic brain injuries (TBI).

Constantine writes: " 'Cleptopolitan' was originally commissioned for performance by Beyond Baroque Literary Arts Center in Venice, California, as part of a new reading series launched in 2017. At the time, I'd just begun conducting workshops for writers living with aphasia, a language processing disorder, which can severely constrain the ability to form or recognize words. The experience did and continues to make me reappraise my relationship to poetry, my absurd privilege, and what it means to identify as an artist. The poem was later published by *Poetry Northwest* in 2023."

ARMEN DAVOUDIAN is the author of *The Palace of Forty Pillars* (Tin House, 2024). He grew up in Isfahan, Iran, and is a PhD candidate in English at Stanford University.

KWAME DAWES is the author of more than thirty books of poetry and prose. His most recent collection, *Sturge Town* (Peepal Tree Press, UK, 2023), is a 2023 PBS Autumn Choice. Dawes is a George W. Holmes University Professor of English and the editor of *Prairie Schooner*. He teaches in the Pacific MFA Program and is the series editor of the African Poetry Book Series; director of the African Poetry Book Fund; and artistic director of the Calabash International Literary Festival. Kwame Dawes is a Fellow of the Royal Society of Literature.

TIMOTHY DONNELLY was born in Providence, Rhode Island, in 1969. He is the author of four books of poetry, including *The Problem of the Many* (Wave Books, 2019); *The Cloud Corporation* (Wave Books, 2010), winner of the 2012 Kingsley Tufts Poetry Award; and, most recently, *Chariot* (Wave Books, 2023). He teaches at Columbia University and lives in Brooklyn.

Donnelly writes: "The poem 'The Bard of Armagh' borrows its end-words from the anglophone version of the traditional Irish ballad of the same name. Although likely to be the work of the Scottish poet Thomas Campbell, the poem is commonly attributed to Patrick Donnelly (1650–1716), an Irish Catholic priest who was made Bishop of Dromore in 1697. When the passing of the Banishment Act of that year sent all 'popish archbishops, bishops, vicars general, deans, Jesuits, monks, friars, and other regular popish clergy' into exile, Donnelly is said to have adopted the persona of a wandering harper named Phelim Brady, the 'Bard of Armagh,' in order to visit members of his diocese in disguise."

RITA DOVE was born in Akron, Ohio, in 1952. She received her BA summa cum laude from Miami University of Ohio in 1973 and her MFA from the University of Iowa in 1977. In 1987, she received the Pulitzer Prize for her third collection of poetry, *Thomas and Beulah* (Carnegie-Mellon University Press), and from 1993 to 1995 she served as U.S. Poet Laureate. Dove has received the 2019 Wallace

Stevens Award; the American Academy of Arts & Letters' 2021 Gold Medal in poetry; the 2022 Ruth Lilly Poetry Prize and 2022 Bobbitt Prize for lifetime achievement from the Library of Congress; and the 2023 medal for distinguished contribution to American letters from the National Book Foundation. She has received both the National Humanities Medal and the National Medal of Arts, making her the only poet ever to receive both. She teaches at the University of Virginia in Charlottesville, where she is the Henry Hoyns Professor of Creative Writing.

Of "Happy End," Dove writes: "When Camille Dungy asked for a contribution to *Orion*'s Fairy Tale issue, I immediately thought of Hansel and Gretel. So many aspects of the story had always bothered me—the father was too meek, the wife too cruel, and at first Hansel had all the good ideas and dominated the action until Gretel engineered their escape. Most vexingly: After being enslaved and caged (not to mention committing murder!), why were these children not traumatized? From the moment I sat down to write and entered their bedroom on that fateful night, strange and powerful forces began tugging at my pen: Gretel grew stronger, her resolve steelier; the witch disappeared—or rather was reincarnated as border control. This contemporary cautionary tale has no Happy End. Even the parents who thought they were sending their children into a brighter future had delivered them—ironically, tragically—to true wolves."

JOANNE DOMINIQUE DWYER was born in Queens, New York. She is the author of *Rasa*, winner of the Marsh Hawk Poetry Prize (2023). Her first book of poems, *Belle Laide*, was published by Sarabande Books in 2013. Dwyer is a recipient of a Rona Jaffe Foundation Writers' Award, an *American Poetry Review* James A. Shestack Prize, and an Anne Halley Prize from the *Massachusetts Review*. She holds an MFA from Warren Wilson's Program for Writers. This is her second appearance in *The Best American Poetry*.

Of "Irish Traveler's Writer's Block" Dwyer writes: "To *tranquilize down* is often a goal of mine and writing itself calms me. It's complicated and it's as simple as a sunrise or the building of a bird's nest. Leonard Cohen's lyrics suggest that one can't depend on anyone or any god. Nevertheless I thought it a worthwhile reason to leave the house: to attend God's funeral."

ELAINE EQUI was born in Oak Park, Illinois, in 1953. She is the author of ten collections of poetry including *Voice-Over* (Coffee House Press, 1998), which was chosen by Thom Gunn for the San Francisco State Poetry Award; *Ripple Effect: New & Selected Poems* (Coffee House Press, 2007); and most recently, *The Intangibles* (Coffee House Press, 2019). A new collection, *Out of the Blank*, is forthcoming in 2025. She was guest editor of *The Best American Poetry 2023*.

Of "Avoidance," Equi writes: "I like the idea that an encounter with a boring book and a forgettable film can somehow lead to a pretty good poem. One evening, my husband and I were watching an old movie on TV. He fell asleep. I tried to read, but finally gave up and moved, in frustration, to a different room where I wrote this rather quickly. Usually, I prefer to write in the morning, before the day's ups and downs take over my brain. This poem is a nice reminder to vary my routine. Sometimes it's easier to catch up with your emotions while they're unfolding rather than recollecting them in tranquility."

Born in Newark, New Jersey, in 1992, GABRIELLA FEE holds a BA from Wellesley College and an MFA from the Writing Seminars at Johns Hopkins University. A recipient of the Elizabeth K. Moser Fund for Poetry Studies Fellowship in 2021 and the Dr. Benjamin J. Sankey Fellowship in Poetry in 2022, Fee is currently a fellow with the Society of Fellows in the Humanities at the Johns Hopkins University.

Of "A Lighthouse Keeper Considers Love," Fee writes: "I grew up near the North Atlantic Coast. I always return to that landscape, and to the figure of the lighthouse keeper, when I think about the solitude, longing, and wildness that characterized my young adulthood. 'A Lighthouse Keeper Considers Love' comes from a series of persona poems in which I write into the perspective of a fictionalized queer woman lighthouse keeper—her history, her attachments, what she notices about the world. This poem is interested in the contradictions of love, its ephemerality and intensity; how enigmatic it is while we keep vigil for it, and how it continues to elude our understanding when it arrives. I used robust internal rhyme and the repetition of 'neither/nor' to give the poem a songlike skeletal structure, but clipped the lines very short to subvert expectations around where that sound and repetition would occur."

BRANDEL FRANCE DE BRAVO was born in 1960 in Washington, D.C., and divides her time between the nation's capital and Mexico. She is the author of *Locomotive Cathedral* (Backwaters Press/University of Nebraska, forthcoming in 2025), *Mother, Loose* (Accents Publishing, 2015), and *Provenance* (Washington Writers' Publishing House, 2008). France de Bravo writes: "'After the Ecstasy, the Laundry' was inspired by a walk through my neighborhood in downtown D.C. and speaks to the varied emotions I often experience in response to change. The poem touches on class/gentrification, my role in it, the scrim of nostalgia, and my attempts to sustain a vision for shared common humanity. If laundry is a humble task, writing is a humbling act. Invariably, I think I've arrived at a brilliant insight (laundry like justice is never over) only to find that I'm the newest, smallest bead on a very long necklace."

DANA GIOIA has published six poetry collections, including *Interrogations at Noon* (Graywolf Press, 2001), which won the American Book Award, and *99 Poems: New & Selected* (Graywolf, 2016), which won the Poets' Prize in 2018. His most recent volume is *Meet Me at the Lighthouse* (Graywolf, 2023). His five critical collections include *Can Poetry Matter?* (Graywolf, 2002) and *Studying with Miss Bishop: Memoirs from a Young Writer's Life* (Paul Dry Books, 2021). He has also written five opera libretti. Gioia served as Chairman of the National Endowment for the Arts from 2003 to 2009 and as California State Poet Laureate from 2015 to 2019. He divides his time between Los Angeles and Sonoma County, California. He was the guest editor of *The Best American Poetry 2018*.

Gioia writes: " 'Satan's Management Style' is an excerpt from a long poem-in-progress, *The Underworld*. This new work describes a living soul who visits the infernal regions, a completely original idea I stole from Dante, Virgil, and Seneca. I hope to finish the poem before I get the opportunity for first-hand observation.

"These stanzas are spoken by the narrator's guide who explains the lack of visible punishments on the crowded streets of Hell. His Satanic Majesty has been a victim of his own success. He has more sinners than demons to handle them. He has solved his management crisis with a sound business strategy. He delegated the details of damnation to the damned. I believe my notion is theologically sound, though the Vatican may disagree.

"The poem is written in asymmetrical seven-line stanzas. They offer the double advantage of being difficult to compose and quietly symbolic. Seven is the mythic number for completion—the Seven Seas, Seven Sacraments, and Seven Deadly Sins. The stanzas reprinted here are spoken on Hell's major shopping street, the Avenue of the Seven Deadly Sins.

"Speaking of sins, I stole two of my best lines from John Milton."

LOUISE GLÜCK was born in New York City in 1943, and died in Cambridge, Massachusetts, in October 2023, three years after she received the Nobel Prize in Literature. She taught at a number of institutions, including Williams College, Stanford, and Yale. Her sixth collection of poems, *The Wild Iris*, published in 1992, won her the Pulitzer Prize and enlarged an already devoted following. Her many later books included the collection *Poems 1962–2012*. She served as Vermont State Poet from 1994 to 1998 and was named Poet Laureate of the United States in 2003. The author of two books of essays on poetry, *Proofs and Theories* and *American Originality*, Glück was the guest editor of *The Best American Poetry 1993*.

Of "Passion and Form," Mary Jo Salter writes: "Louise Glück, nine years younger than her close friend Mark Strand, died as he did at the age of eighty. Since they both appear in this year's *Best American Poetry*, and both were guest editors of previous volumes, it is worth noting their mutual respect, and also how different are the poems they chose by one another. Glück selected three sections from Strand's long, philosophical poem in tercets, *Dark Harbor*; Strand opted for a rather conversational poem by Glück, 'Celestial Music,' on a serious subject, her inability to believe in heaven. Glück's free verse poem is shapely in argument, and indeed it concludes, 'The love of form is a love of endings.' Glück often expressed a desire to be surprised; she wrote of her work as an editor, 'my hope was to have my mind changed,' and that was evident within her poetry too. As 2023 began, I came across 'Passion and Form' in *The Threepenny Review* and knew right away that I wanted it for this book; it was the first poem I chose. Its brevity is one form of surprise, as is the sweetness of the poem's one rhyme, kissed / unnoticed, which of course is noticed by the reader with pure delight."

AMY GLYNN is a poet and essayist whose work appears widely in journals and anthologies including *The Best American Poetry* (2010, 2012). She was the inaugural Poet Laureate for the cities of Lafayette and Orinda, California. She lives in the San Francisco Bay Area.

Of "Space Is the Final Frontier," Glynn writes: "Richard Kenney's epigraph (from *The Invention of the Zero*) connected the dots to a 'final form' for this poem after I'd tried several approaches that didn't work. The title, from the title sequence of *Star Trek*, refers to psychological 'space' in the aftermath of an imploded relationship. Allusions to things being 'written in the stars,' or otherwise attributing human phenomena to the transits of celestial bodies are common to virtually every time and every culture, suggesting that there's either some validity to the idea or at least that humans have a strong innate drive to assign meaning to recurring patterns. Even people with no belief in fate or destiny often have the experience of meeting someone and having the eerie feeling that they already know them, that they are connected by some invisible thread—whatever is responsible for it, I find that phenomenon equally delightful and disconcerting. And occasionally kind of devastating."

JESSICA GREENBAUM was born in Brooklyn in 1957. She grew up in Long Island, attended Barnard College, was in the inaugural class of the University of Houston's writing program, and finally moved back to Brooklyn in 1987. Her first book, *Inventing Difficulty*, came out from Silverfish Review Press' Gerald Cable Prize; her second, *The Two Yvonnes*, was chosen by Paul Muldoon for the Princeton University Press and was named a Best Book of the Year by *Library Journal*. The University of Pittsburgh Press published her most recent book, *Spilled and Gone*, which was named by *The Boston Globe* as a best book of 2021. With Rabbi Hara Person, she coedited *Mishkan HaSeder*, the first-ever poetry Haggadah. A recipient of awards from the National Endowment of the Arts and the Poetry Society of America, she teaches inside and outside academia, and is a licensed social worker.

Of "Each Other Moment," Greenbaum writes: "As a narrative, autobiographical poet, my most used pronoun would have to be 'I'; thank goodness this poem was influenced by my friend Alice Elliott Dark's short story 'Rumm Road,' written in the first-person plural. I remember feeling the power of her speaker voicing the experience of a time, and if you are in your sixties sitting with your sister-in-law on a hot summer day in New York City trying to order an ice tea but having trouble capturing the necessary QR code—while people who would formerly be actual waitstaff taking your order are walking around delivering drinks to other more nimble customers—the zeitgeist comes after you before the first sip. Some days it's a short hop from restaurant devolution to the earth's wholesale demise."

Born in New York City in 1948, RACHEL HADAS is the author of numerous books of poetry, essays, memoir, and translation. Her most recent books are prose selections *Piece by Piece* (Paul Dry Books, 2021) and three poetry collections: *Love and Dread* (Measure Press, Inc., 2021), *Pandemic Almanac* (Ragged Sky Press, 2022), and *Ghost Guest* (Ragged Sky Press, 2023). Her new book, *From Which We Start Awake*, a prosimetrum alternating poems and prose, is forthcoming from Able Muse Press in 2025. She is the recipient of honors and awards including a Guggenheim Fellowship in poetry and the O.B. Hardison Award in poetry from the Folger Shakespeare Library, and is one of forty translators of Nonnus's rollicking forty-eight–book epic from late antiquity, *Tales of Dionysus* (University of Michigan Press, 2022). She recently retired from Rutgers-Newark, where she taught for many years.

Hadas writes: "I can identify four strands or ingredients that went to make up 'Voyage' and that I can discern in the poem: dream; memory; fragments of canonical poems I know and love; and a phase of my own life. Briefly, the imagery of the crowded ship, the groups on the piers, even the bouquets and patent leather shoes, all derive from a vivid dream. But the dream seemed to refer to the time many years ago when I lived on a Greek island and did indeed sail between islands on crowded ferries: hence memory too played a role. The italicized lines come respectively from Asia's song 'My soul is an enchanted boat' in Shelley's *Prometheus Unbound* and from the passage in Wordsworth's Immortality Ode that refers to the imitative play of young children.

"It has become a tiresome commonplace to refer to almost any stage, phase, process, or passage in life as a 'journey.' Perhaps 'Voyage' is a slightly more evocative term for what is often called moving on.

There's a certain pathos about those landmarks bobbing in the wake of the ongoing vessel—that's how the dream seemed to refer to a passage in my life.

"Finally, 'Voyage,' which went through many revisions and cuts (at one time the poem was much longer and in tercets), remains something of a mystery to me: vivid, I hope, but not transparent. Like a dream."

SASKIA HAMILTON (1967–2023) was the author of five collections of poetry: *As for Dream, Divide These, Corridor, Canal: New and Selected Poems,* and *All Souls,* all published by Graywolf Press except *Canal* (Arc Publications). She was the editor of several volumes of poetry and letters, including *The Letters of Robert Lowell,* and was the coeditor of *Words in Air: The Complete Correspondence Between Elizabeth Bishop and Robert Lowell.* Her edition of *The Dolphin Letters, 1970–1979: Elizabeth Hardwick, Robert Lowell, and Their Circle* received the Pegasus Award for Poetry Criticism from the Poetry Foundation and the Morton N. Cohen Award for a Distinguished Edition of Letters from the Modern Language Association. She was also the recipient of an Arts and Letters Award in Literature from the American Academy of Arts and Letters. She taught for many years at Barnard College.

Maya C. Popa writes: "As is true of many of the poems in Hamilton's posthumous *All Souls,* this lyric sequence is written in the shadow of cancer treatments that muddle and challenge linear thinking. Hamilton delivers and transforms this hardship on the page, revealing its aesthetic and existential questions as memory, perspective, and language meet in surprising and moving ways. Through its evocative lyric leaps, the poem makes luminous connections among moments, places, and writers."

JEFFREY HARRISON was born in Cincinnati, Ohio, in 1957. His books of poetry include *The Singing Underneath* (Dutton, 1988), a National Poetry Series winner; *Between Lakes* (Four Way Books, 2020); and *Into Daylight* (Tupelo Press, 2014), winner of the Dorset Prize. He has received fellowships from the Guggenheim Foundation, the National Endowment for the Arts, and the Bogliasco Foundation. His essay "The Story of a Box," about Marcel Duchamp and his family, was published in *The Common* in 2023. He lives in the Boston area.

Of "A Message from Tony Hoagland," Harrison writes: "I first met Tony Hoagland in 1984, when both of us were waiters at Bread Loaf. I look back at that time fondly, but this poem is not an example of emotion recollected in tranquility. Receiving an email from Tony a year after his death was so startling that it immediately triggered the poem. The last few lines refer to D. H. Lawrence's 'Snake,' but I was also thinking of Tony's poem 'Lawrence,' which characterizes his eponymous subject in words that now might also seem to describe himself: 'a man who burned like an acetylene torch / from one end to the other of his life.' "

TERRANCE HAYES's recent publications—*So to Speak*, a collection of poems, and *Watch Your Language*, a collection of visual and lyric essays—were concurrently released by Penguin Books in 2023. He has received the National Book Award for poetry, the Poetry Foundation Pegasus Award for Poetry Criticism, and fellowships from the Guggenheim Foundation and the MacArthur Foundation. He is a professor at New York University. He was the guest editor of *The Best American Poetry 2014*.

Of "How to Fold," Hayes writes: "I like to take my time wrestling a poem, carrying it through the day like a puzzle. It's a good way to spend the time. However, this one unfolded so quickly I hardly recall writing it. It's something of a gift and mystery to me."

JOHN HENNESSY was born in Philadelphia in 1965 and grew up in New Jersey. He is the author of three collections, the latest being *Bridge and Tunnel* (Turning Point, 2007). With Ostap Kin he translated *A New Orthography* (Lost Horse Press, 2020), the selected poems of Serhiy Zhadan, and the anthology *Babyn Yar: Ukrainian Poets Respond* (Harvard Library of Ukrainian Literature/HUP, 2023). *Set Change*, Andrukhovych's selected poems, is forthcoming from New York Review Books. Hennessy is the poetry editor of *The Common* and teaches at the University of Massachusetts, Amherst.

Hennessy writes: "I spent a long time looking for the poem inside the moment expanded in 'Domestic Retrograde.' In the end it proved helpful to reconsider the pronouns: a shift there helped both to clarify and complicate everything around the bird's strange arrival in our kitchen."

W. J. HERBERT's debut collection, *Dear Specimen* (Beacon Press, 2021), was selected by Kwame Dawes as a winner of the 2020 National Poetry Series and was awarded a 2022 Maine Literary Award for poetry.

Of "Pando's Grove," Herbert writes, "When the breeze kicks up along the Fishlake Scenic Byway, Utah's Highway 25, Pando's heart-shaped leaves murmur above its trunks' watchful eyes. Born near the end of the last ice age, the 106-acre clonal aspen colony is one of the world's largest living organisms, with nearly 50,000 DNA-identical trees. Pando suffers from overgrazing, disease, and climate-induced drought, but as the wind quivers through each leaf, it breathes."

RICHIE HOFMANN was born in Silver Spring, Maryland, in 1987. He is the author of two collections of poems, *A Hundred Lovers* (Knopf, 2022) and *Second Empire* (Alice James Books, 2015). His poetry has been honored with a Ruth Lilly Fellowship from the Poetry Foundation and a Wallace Stegner Fellowship from Stanford University.

Of "Lamb" Hofmann writes: "This poem is inspired by an important figure in my childhood—my poor stuffed animal, who got so beat up being dragged around Europe. It might have been a calf (its name was Moo-Moo) after all. I have many happy memories of traveling with it, but reflecting many years later, I think the stuffed animal also suggests to me the sense that even in childhood, maybe especially in childhood, we are subject to a world of threat, responsibility, and loss."

MARIE HOWE was born in Rochester, New York, in 1950. She has published four books of poems, as well as *New and Selected Poems* (W. W. Norton, 2024). She has been New York State Poet and a chancellor of the Academy of American poets. At present she is Poet-in-Residence at the Cathedral Church of St. John the Divine in New York City.

Of "Chainsaw," Howe writes: "I was teaching a class with the wonderful Laurie Wagner in San Miguel, Mexico. Laurie gave writing prompts in the morning and I suggested revision techniques in the afternoon. This particular morning there was, in fact, a chainsaw (there's always a chainsaw somewhere), and that started the poem that led me where I did not expect to go."

OMOTARA JAMES is the author of the poetry collection *Song of My Softening* (Alice James Books, 2024). Born in London, in 1984, she is the daughter of Nigerian and Trinidadian immigrants. Her work has received support from the African Poetry Book Fund, the Poetry Foundation, the Academy of American Poets, the New York Foundation for the Arts, Lambda Literary, and the Cave Canem Foundation. She edits and teaches poetry in New York City.

Of "Closure," James writes: "This poem explores how we carry and make space for the competing natures of our personal and family histories. I attempt to examine the relationship among closure, courage, memory, and time. As a construct, closure serves to separate the present moment from the past, in order to create emotional distance, whereas courage bears the truth of the present moment without looking away. So too is the poet compelled to look at a thing straight-on, even as she tells it slant. Therefore, the poet carries and confronts the truth of the past, as she carries and confronts the truth of the present."

EVE JONES was born in St. Louis, Missouri, in 1976. She is the author of *Bird in the Machine* (Turning Point, 2010), and her poems and photographs have been published widely. She taught creative writing for many years in Lindenwood University's MFA in Writing program, and currently lives in Northeast Florida, near the sea.

Jones writes: "The conundrum of introducing 'Japan' is real, and at the end of the day I admit I'm left only with questions: What is this thing in me that rushes to assure the reader that the poem is only partially *true*? Is disconnection a kind of death? Is a sister on the other side of the world a *sister*? If human beings save each other all the time, and we do, why are there specific instances in which it is impossible? And who is the disconnected one? Etc."

GEORGE KALOGERIS was born in Lynn, Massachusetts, in 1955. His most recent book of poems is *Winthropos* (Louisiana State University, 2021). He is also the author of *Guide to Greece* (LSU, 2018), *Dialogos: Paired Poems in Translation*, and poems based on the notebooks of Albert Camus, *Camus: Carnets*. His poems and translations have been anthologized in *Joining Music with Reason* (Waywiser, 2010), chosen by Christopher Ricks. He is the winner of the James Dickey Poetry Prize, the Stephen J. Meringoff Award, and the Sheila Margaret Motton Prize.

Of "Byzantine Chanting," Kalogeris writes: "My poem is based upon a childhood memory of the cantor in our Greek Orthodox church in Lynn, Massachusetts. I had heard from my parents that he was a refugee from Smyrna and knew that he also happened to work in one of the factories down the street from the church. Although I had only the faintest inkling of what my relatives called the *Catastrophe* (the burning of the Greek section of Smyrna by the Turks in 1922, and the massive population displacement in its aftermath), Lynn was famous at the time for its billowing shoe factories, and somehow the constant smell of burning leather activated my imagination—as if I had caught a faint whiff of smoldering Smyrna. Early on I was a devoted reader of myths, and in my illustrated childhood text Arion was pictured in his majestic 'singing robes.'"

STEPHEN KAMPA was born in Missoula, Montana, in 1981 and grew up in Daytona Beach, Florida. He is the author of four collections of poetry: *Cracks in the Invisible* (Ohio University Press, 2011), *Bachelor Pad* (Waywiser, 2014), *Articulate as Rain* (Waywiser, 2018), and *World Too Loud to Hear* (Able Muse, 2023). He has also been a regular session musician for WildRoots Records. He currently teaches at Flagler College in Saint Augustine, Florida.

Of "Someone Else's Gift," Kampa writes: "While much ink has been spilled in the service of encouraging us to accept ourselves with all of our flaws, I feel less has been said about accepting ourselves with all of our gifts. It's more difficult than it seems. Sometimes, we want just a little bit more giftedness: a guitar player who can play absolutely anything on guitar insists he should also be an actor, an actor who has achieved unimaginable fame as an actor insists she must publish a book of poems, the poet who writes exquisitely shaped lyrics insists she would rather be a novelist, the novelist who has broken a million hearts insists he would be happier drawing cartoons. I have come to two conclusions: (1) it is harder to accept ourselves than we think, and (2) we can always find new ways to be greedy.

"I once worked with a singer who loved early roots and blues music and wanted more than anything to be the next Empress of the Blues. One night at a gig, someone in the audience asked if she would sing opera, for which she had been classically trained. She silenced the entire bar in three seconds flat. And then we went ahead and played blues for the rest of the night."

RICHARD KENNEY was born in Glens Falls, New York, in 1948. His most recent book is *Terminator: Poems 2008–2018* (Knopf, 2019).

Of "Self's the Man," Kenney writes: "Maybe I should have called this something else. Philip Larkin thought the title up; I just borrowed it because it makes me smile. Larkin wrote a humorous verse about the relative selfishness of married men and bachelors. I suppose I wrote interrogatory verse about the unnerving selflessness of most of what we do. Is Self really just a color commentator on what its animal's already doing? The Libet Experiment? Knock-Knock?"

KARL KIRCHWEY was born in Boston in 1956. He is the author of seven books of poems; his eighth, entitled *Good Apothecary*, is forthcoming from Northwestern University Press. He has edited *Poems of Rome* (Knopf, 2018) and *Poems of Healing* (Knopf, 2021), and his translation of Paul Verlaine's book appeared as *Poems Under Saturn*. He has been working on a book-length hybrid memoir about war and memory called *A Boy Falling Out of the Sky: One Family's History of Ambiguous Loss*, individual essays from which have appeared in *AGNI*, *The American Scholar*, *The Hudson Review*, and *Raritan*. Kirchwey is Professor of English and Creative Writing at Boston University, where he teaches in the MFA program in creative writing.

Of "*Kiss Me Deadly* (1955)," Kirchwey writes: "Like many other people, my wife and I are great followers of *noir* films, and the pandemic lockdown carried our enthusiasm to new heights. In connection with a family memoir I was working on, we also watched a large number of mostly second-rate WWII movies set in the Pacific Theater. At some point, I detected a pattern beginning to emerge, inasmuch as a number of the films we were watching had elements of the Classical mythology incongruously woven through them.

"This happened for the first time in a WWII submarine movie called *Operation Pacific* (1951) starring John Wayne and Patricia Neal. It seemed to me that, since it was made during the Korean War, those involved with the film might have been a bit more resistant to swaggering heroics. My wife and I had settled in to wait out the inevitable victory, when something remarkable happened: the screenwriter and director George Waggner inserted into the dialogue the prophecy of a peaceful death given to Odysseus by Tiresias, who in Book XI of the *Odyssey* says the hero must walk inland carrying an oar on his shoulder until it is mistaken for a winnowing fan by those he meets, at which point he is to plant the oar in the earth and make an offering to Poseidon, the god of the sea.

"Sometime later, we watched a movie called *White Heat* (1949) in which Jimmy Cagney plays the part of Arthur 'Cody' Jarrett, a gangster and killer with a crush on his mother. He and his gang hit upon the idea of hiding inside an empty gasoline truck in order to infiltrate and rob a factory; apparently this inspiration derives from Jarrett's 'Ma' telling him the story of the Trojan Horse when he was a child. Finally, we found our way to *Kiss Me Deadly* (1955), based on the Mickey Spillane crime novel of the same title. The movie, a parable for the age of nuclear dread and Cold War almost on a par with *Fail Safe* or *Dr. Strangelove*, roughly concerns the theft and commerce of radioactive material, and here the operative myth is that of Pandora's Box, by which evil is released into the world because of human curiosity.

"Eventually it seemed to me that the three poems resulting from these movies made a trilogy, and I gathered them under a single title deriving from a remark—delivered, it is to be assumed, with the deepest irony—by a character in *White Heat*, who says: 'We might all profit by a closer study of classical literature.'"

YUSEF KOMUNYAKAA was born in Bogalusa, Louisiana, in 1947. His most recent collection, *Everyday Mojo Songs of Earth: New and Selected Poems*, was published by Farrar, Straus and Giroux in 2021. He recently retired from teaching in the creative writing program at New York University. In 2021 he received the Zbigniew Herbert International Poetry Award. He was the guest editor of *The Best American Poetry 2003*.

DAVID LEHMAN is the series editor of *The Best American Poetry*.

Of "Ithaca," Lehman writes: "I spend much of my time in Ithaca, New York, and reread the *Odyssey* every year. In March 2012, I must have had an unconscious premonition of the cancer that would afflict me in 2013 and dominate my life for the next four years. With a burst of energy and ambition, I gave myself an assignment: write drafts of thirty sonnets, with occasional rhymes, raising ultimate questions. I chose for an epigraph a famous line in a sonnet by Joachim du Bellay (c. 1522–1560): *Heureux qui, comme Ulysse, a fait un beau voyage.* A rough rendering gives us "Happy the man who, like Ulysses, has made a glorious voyage,' losing the magic of 'un beau voyage.' I began my first sonnet with 'Happy as Ulysses is he who ventures forth' and, throughout the sequence, used variants of 'Happy as Ulysses' and 'What did he believe in?' as leitmotifs. I completed a draft of thirty sonnets in 2013, then suspended working on it during the cancer ordeal. A few years ago, I resumed tinkering with the sequence. Not until 2022 did I regard it as provisionally finished. I am grateful to Paula Dietz and the other editors at *The Hudson Review* who published this excerpt from 'Ithaca.' "

ADA LIMÓN is the author of six books of poetry, including *The Carrying* (Milkweed Editions, 2018), which won the National Book Critics Circle Award for Poetry. Her most recent collection, *The Hurting Kind* (2022), was shortlisted for the Griffin Poetry Prize. She is the 24th Poet Laureate of the United States and the recipient of a MacArthur Fellowship. As the Poet Laureate, her signature project is called *You Are Here* and focuses on how poetry can help connect us to the natural world. Limón is the editor of *You Are Here: Poetry in the Natural World*, published by Milkweed Editions in association with the Library of Congress in 2024.

Of "In Praise of Mystery: A Poem for Europa," Limón writes: "When NASA first asked if I'd be interested in making a poem that would go with the Europa Clipper spacecraft to the second moon of Jupiter, I immediately said yes. But as soon as I got off the phone, my heart sank. I rarely do occasional poems and have very little experience with writing poems 'for' something. I realized the only way into the poem was to allow myself a 'we' (another thing I rarely do). This poem had to be larger than an 'I,' and I hope it feels that way. I was moved to tears to have it included here. I wanted first and foremost to make a good and honest poem."

SARAH LUCZAJ, PhD, born in England in 1970, is a writer, therapist, translator, and visual artist who lives between Glasgow, UK, and rural southeastern Poland, where she is the cofounder of the terrealuma healing refuge. Her poems and translations have appeared in many journals, including *The American Poetry Review*, *Modern Poetry in Translation*, and *AGNI* online. Sarah is the author of *An Urgent Request*

(Fortunate Daughter Press, 2009), as well as the English translations in dual-language collections by Polish poets Grażyna Wojcieszko and Ida Sieciechowicz, and the unpublished poetry collection *64 Changes*. Inventor of the Creative Regeneration process and author of *Creative Regeneration* (Wayward Publications, 2019), she is currently working on *Felt Senses of Self and No Self: At the Intersections of Therapy, Focusing, and Buddhism*. She loves running Creative Regeneration workshops and retreats in nature, facilitating meditation, focusing, freewriting, and intuitive painting. She has two daughters.

Luczaj writes: " 'Shopping Lists' was written in spring 2022, shortly after Russia's invasion of Ukraine. I was in Poland at the time, and I wrote it on the balcony of my poet friend Cecilia Woloch's flat, sitting at a table literally strewn with shopping lists scrawled in my own hand, few of which I could understand myself. Through the terrealuma healing refuge, I was collecting money and buying medical supplies, according to lists sent to me in various languages by my friend in Ukraine. The everyday closeness of our contact and the stark and utter difference between our experiences was striking to me. The poem is, however, mainly about technology, logic, and measurement, the strength, reliability, almost invincibility of those systems and at the same time their complete inadequacy. I hoped to create a palpable sense of everything that could not be measured, and hence is missing, even from the language I use. That 'everything' is an understanding that can only be put into the system by human beings. The same human beings who are killing and looting, and shopping. So where is it? The uncapturable is poetry."

AMIT MAJMUDAR is the author of *What He Did in Solitary: Poems* (Knopf, 2020), *Twin A: A Memoir* (Slant Books, 2023), *Black Avatar and Other Essays* (Acre Books, 2023), *The Great Game* (Acre Books, 2024), and the hybrid work *Three Metamorphoses* (Orison Books, 2024), as well as a new poetry collection to be published by Knopf in 2026. His state's former first Poet Laureate, he works as a diagnostic radiologist in Westerville, Ohio, where he lives with his wife and three children.

Of "Charmed Life," Majmudar writes: " 'Count no man lucky until he is dead,' said Solon, a lawgiver in ancient Greece. You never know when a friendly universe might turn on you: The monthlong dry cough that turns out to be a lung mass, the backache that turns out to be a bone metastasis; a quick trip in the car to get bread and bananas that takes a left at the light into lifelong quadriplegia. Just days before that catastrophe: A wedding, or a book deal, or a Disney trip with the kids. . . . It's not a tightly enforced law, but things do tend to cancel out when it comes to good luck and bad luck, good times and bad times. (At least that holds for those of us who crowd the middle of the luck distribution; certainly some people at either extreme have only one sort of luck in abundance.)

"This dashed-off charm of a poem, 'Charmed Life,' reflects that sense of yin and yang, of scooping slop and caviar with the same spoon. The speaker plays life on easy mode until that turn at the end, but the first word of the last line embeds the idea. 'Nemesis' comes from the Greek for giving someone what they deserve, and before that, from the Indo-European root *nem-*, which means 'distribute.' Everyone deserves trial and triumph in roughly equal measures. And for the most part, that is what we get."

CLARENCE MAJOR was born in Atlanta, Georgia, in 1936. *Four Days in Algeria*, his forthcoming collection of poetry, will be published by Red Hen Press (2025). He is author of sixteen previous collections, thirteen novels, three volumes of short stories, and ten works of nonfiction. His work was selected for inclusion in *The Best American Poetry 2019*. Before retiring in 2007 as distinguished professor in the English department, University of California, Davis, he taught at Sarah Lawrence College, University of Washington, Howard University, Temple University, University of California at San Diego, and the University of Nice, France. Clarence Major lives in northern California.

Major writes: "'Weather Conditions' came to me one morning while listening to the weather report. I realized I had heard something like the phrase, 'For your local weather, here is a quick peek out your window,' many times. It had become so familiar that I had not thought about what it really meant. The poem evolved from that moment. Before hearing any weather report, I often get up and walk to the window and look out to see what I call 'the day.' In other words, to see whether it is going to be sunny or cloudy or foggy or raining, but doing so is never prompted by listening to the weather report. Somehow the two never connect. But I've long thought about the art of the window as metaphor and vehicle. It frames its subject while at the same time representing it indifferently. As vehicle the window is both active and passive. But what does one see when one looks out any window? Name your subject, complete with things loaded with narrative elements or symbolism or the abstraction of weather. The possibility of also exploring things beyond what is seen can be endless. These things became the impetus for the poem."

CHARLES MARTIN was born in 1942 in the Bronx. He has received the Harold Morton Landon Award from the Academy of American Poets and an award for literature from the American Academy of Arts and Letters. His most recent books of poems are *Signs & Wonders* (2011) and *Future Perfect* (2018), both published by Johns Hopkins University Press. His version of Euripides's *Medea* was published in 2019 by the University of California Press.

Martin writes: "We tend to be possessive about the poems we write. Blame it, if you will, on Horace, who may have set us down that trail by saying of his own work, 'This monument that I have raised will outlast even bronze. . . .' There's an alternative tradition that sees poetry as dialogic, communal, less defended, and ongoing, a process rather than a monument. 'You Summon Me . . .' is an attempt at exploring that alternative view."

HEATHER MCHUGH lives on the Olympic Peninsula and takes on a few private manuscript evaluations every year (inquiries at postcocious@gmail.com). She's working on a second and final essay collection comprising a lifetime's lectures.

McHugh writes: "'Two Widows, Making a Bed' is an impertinent impersonation."

MAGGIE MILLNER is the author of *Couplets* (Farrar, Straus and Giroux, 2023). She works as a lecturer at Yale and a senior editor at *The Yale Review*.

Millner writes: "These poems have been excerpted from a book-length, narrative poem about love, queerness, heartbreak, and constraint. The book's prosodic rules, based on a loose interpretation of the heroic couplet, formalize the speaker's competing obsessions with control and submission. In this sense, it is a poem explicitly interested in dualities—not only those thematic binaries related to gender and romantic coupledom, but also those that haunt and animate all makers of poems: verse and prose; constraint and freedom; lyric and narrative; me and you."

ANGE MLINKO was born in Philadelphia in 1969. She is the author of six books of poetry, most recently *Venice* (Farrar, Straus and Giroux, 2022), and a book of lyric criticism, *Difficult Ornaments: Florida and the Poets* (Oxford University Press, 2024). She has won the Randall Jarrell Award in Criticism, the Frederick Bock Prize, and a Guggenheim Fellowship. She teaches poetry at the University of Florida.

Mlinko writes: " 'The Open C' was written on St. George Island, on the Florida Gulf Coast. It's impossible not to gaze at the horizon of the sea without thinking of the Chicxulub Crater. The sonnet plays on the letter *C*, sea, and what you can and can't see, including your own face. 'Compact' may mean agreement, density, or the little compact with two mirrors. The extinction that awaits may be someone else's, or it may be your own."

ANDREW MOTION (born in London, England, in 1952) was the United Kingdom Poet Laureate from 1999 to 2009 and is the cofounder of The Poetry Archive. His most recent collection is *Waders* (McSweeney's, 2024). Since 2015 he has lived in the United States, where he is Homewood Professor of the Arts at Johns Hopkins University in Baltimore.

Motion writes: "I was raised in the English countryside, and 'The Explanation' remembers an incident from my childhood in which a boy slightly older than myself brought over some ferrets to reduce the rabbit population that was laying waste to my father's vegetable garden. The rabbits met a violent end, but the evidence for this (and other matters contingent) was all heard, not seen—as the poem explains."

PAUL MULDOON was born in County Armagh in 1951. He now lives in New York. A former radio and television producer for the BBC in Belfast, he has taught at Princeton University for thirty-five years. He is the author of fifteen collections of poetry including *Joy in Service on Rue Tagore*, published by FSG and Faber and Faber in 2024. He received the 2003 Pulitzer Prize. A fellow of the Royal Society for

Literature and a fellow of the American Academy of Arts and Letters, he was guest editor of *The Best American Poetry 2005*.

Of "Joy in Service on Rue Tagore," Muldoon writes: "This poem seems to want to combine the tradition of the espionage thriller with the somewhat more mundane aspects of advancing age—mostly the endless visits to far-flung medical practices. The character of Emile may well be a double agent of the kind to which we've become all too familiar from the 'dirty war' in my native Northern Ireland, though the detail of 'the hand he kept in the fridge' derives from the exploits of the Westies, the Irish-American gang that once flourished in Hell's Kitchen. The title, by the way, is an ironic take on a quote from the great Indian poet Rabindranath Tagore: 'I slept and dreamt that life was joy. I awoke and saw that life was service. I acted and behold, service was joy.'"

HARRYETTE MULLEN's books include *Recyclopedia* (Graywolf Press, 2006), winner of a PEN Beyond Margins Award, and *Sleeping with the Dictionary* (University of California, 2002). A collection of essays and interviews, *The Cracks Between What We Are and What We Are Supposed to Be* (University of Alabama, 2012), won an Elizabeth Agee Prize. Graywolf published *Urban Tumbleweed: Notes from a Tanka Diary* in 2013.

Mullen writes: "I began writing 'Haiku Garden' during a period of relative isolation when the pandemic lockdown required working from home, teaching classes, and attending meetings and events remotely. Hours spent staring at a screen were relieved by walks on the beach or on canyon trails, and small gatherings with friends, neighbors, and colleagues in backyards, gardens, public parks, outdoor cafés, and restaurant courtyards. Haiku and short prose pieces written during that time are collected in *Open Leaves*. Like my previous book, *Urban Tumbleweed*, it was inspired by walking and hiking in and around Los Angeles, contemplating the beauty, diversity, and fragility of life."

JESSE NATHAN was born in Berkeley, California, in 1983, and was raised there and in rural Kansas. He is the author of *Eggtooth* (Unbound Edition Press, 2023). He has published translations of the *Popol Vuh*, as well as work by Alfonsina Storni and Brenda Solís-Fong. His writing has been supported by fellowships from the Andrew W. Mellon Foundation, the Ashbery Home School, the Kansas Arts Commission,

Stanford University, and the Arts Research Center at the University of California, Berkeley.

Of "Dame's Rocket," Nathan writes: "A few years ago I spent the spring living on the land I grew up on, a grain farm in rural Kansas and the surrounding watershed. After many years of being away, I got to see the flowers come in their sequence, in waves. I spent a lot of time in those months wandering alone in the creeks and pastures, old cemeteries and roads. I got to know the place again. Saw much beauty in the present and past of it, and also much human sadness. Saw that it was part of me, and I was part of it, always, whether I wanted it or not. That year I was working on a typewriter, and I noticed how working that way affected lines and rhythms. I wrote shorter poems. I wrote the first drafts of this one on it. My memory is that it was twice as long at first."

JACQUELINE OSHEROW was born in Philadelphia in 1956. Her ninth collection of poems, *Divine Ratios*, in which "Fast Track: Beijing, Montana, Harlem" appears, was published by LSU Press in 2023. She has received grants from the John Simon Guggenheim Memorial Foundation and Ingram Merrill Foundation, the NEA, and the Witter Bynner Poetry Prize from the American Academy and Institute of Arts and Letters. Her poems have appeared in *The Best American Poetry* (1996, 1998, and 2018). She is Distinguished Professor of English at the University of Utah.

Of "Fast Track: Beijing, Montana, Harlem," Osherow writes: "This poem was begun in the summer of 2016, at the University of Utah's Taft-Nicholson Center in Montana's Centennial Valley, a remote spot reached on a dirt road that has no cell phone service. I was nonetheless able to Skype there with my daughter, who had only just recently arrived in China. That strange conjunction, crowded Beijing and empty Montana, was my starting point. I'm not sure I had any idea where the poem would go. It was only after I'd spent a few days on the East Coast, en route to Europe on sabbatical, that the poem took off. I worked on it on planes, trains, the Greyhound Philadelphia Express mentioned in the poem, and completed it in Berlin in October. I love writing about one place in another; it's what one remembers—rather than what one is looking at—that, for me at least, becomes the stuff of poems. I'm not sure when this turned into a poem about staying put and paying attention, but I've always loved Paul Celan's definition of poems as 'gifts to the attentive.' Poems are also products of attention. And the work of Dickinson—a poet who has meant so much to me since I was a young adolescent—demonstrates that one needn't experience a large swath of the world to write great poems. Indeed, what she accomplished from the vantage point of a single window in a single room has always made me feel like a bit of a fraud, writing, as I do, so many poems about various sites around the world."

Rowan Ricardo Phillips is the author of seven previous books of poetry, prose, and translation. The recipient of a Whiting Award, a Guggenheim Fellowship, the Anisfield-Wolf Book Award, the PEN/ESPN Award for Literary Sports Writing, the Nicolás Guillén Outstanding Book Award, the PEN/Joyce Osterweil Award, and the GLCA New Writers Award, Phillips is a Distinguished Professor of English at Stony Brook University and the poetry editor of *The New Republic*. His book in progress, *I Just Want Them to Remember Me: Black Baseball in America* will be published by Farrar, Straus and Giroux in 2025. He lives in New York City and Barcelona.

Phillips writes: "This poem has a twin, also entitled 'The First and Final Poem Is the Sun,' in which the lines of this poem are reversed. The two poems open and conclude my fourth collection, *Silver* (Farrar, Straus and Giroux, 2024)."

Robert Pinsky was born in 1940, in Long Branch, New Jersey. His recent autobiography is *Jersey Breaks: Becoming an American Poet* (W. W. Norton, 2022). His new PoemJazz album *Proverbs of Limbo* is available on Spotify, Apple Music, and Amazon Music, and his book of poems of the same title was recently published by Farrar, Straus and Giroux. Pinsky's earlier books of poetry include *Gulf Music* (FSG, 2007) and his translation *The Inferno of Dante* (FSG, 1994). He was the guest editor of *The Best of the Best American Poetry: 25th Anniversary Edition*.

Of "Proverbs of Limbo," Pinsky writes, "'Proverbs of Limbo' is the title track for a words-with-music album and the title poem for a book: two efforts to approach in a fresh way the fraught subject of borders and the in-between (the root meaning of 'limbo'). The jagged, contrary 'Proverbs of Hell' by William Blake have their troublemaker say in the borderlands between violently clashing theocracies of his time. I find a less judgmental borderland in the Buddhist idea of the ordinary as a terrain for enlightenment. So, 'The Buddha is a liquor store / On a busy corner.' An ordinary retail good? An addictive exploitation? Or everything in between?"

MAYA C. POPA was born in New York in 1989. She is the author of *Wound Is the Origin of Wonder* (W. W. Norton, 2022) and *American Faith* (Sarabande Books, 2019). She is the poetry reviews editor at *Publishers Weekly* and teaches poetry at New York University.

Of "What's Unsaid," Popa writes: "I spent July 2022 in a small village in the mountains of the Peloponnese called Vamvakou. My husband and I would sometimes drive down the mountain at sunset to visit Sparta, the closest city an hour from the village. The drives were quiet, remote, exquisitely beautiful, with wind farms turning silently in the distance. The area was known for its jackals and wild boars, which I only saw once. The experience was as mesmerizing as the poem suggests."

The child of Sri Lankan Tamils, VIDYAN RAVINTHIRAN grew up in Leeds (in the north of England) and now teaches at Harvard. He has published three works of criticism, edited multiple books of South Asian verse (most recently, with Seni Seneviratne and Shash Trevett, the first-ever anthology of Sri Lankan poetry), and written two collections of poetry—both from Bloodaxe Books in the United Kingdom, *Grun-tu-molani* and *The Million-Petalled Flower of Being Here*. His next book will be a combination of poetry criticism and memoir, *Asian/Other*, to be published in the United States by Norton in 2025.

Ravinthiran writes: " 'Eelam' was the separate homeland for Tamils, dreamed of by the LTTE—the Tamil Tigers—who, opposing Sri Lanka's repressive Sinhala-Buddhist government, also killed many innocent people. Civilians were murdered by both sides.

"My parents moved to England in the 1970s. We are a supremely anxious family, and some of this comes, no doubt, of being a minority within a minority within a minority—what I have designated elsewhere a *hyperminority*—once subjected to state-mandated genocide. But that anxiety trickles down to the most trivial things.

"In therapy we're often asked to challenge perspectives inherited from our parents. One reason this is so hard is because it seems to mean dismissing as invalid much of *their* lives. We go on behaving as they did, to keep insisting on the reality of their concerns. To change ourselves, must we betray them? And for the immigrant, whose connection to a storied and tortured past may be experienced primarily *as* that undercurrent, or persisting thread, of anxiety—am I being unhistorical, vapid, in choosing against inherited traumas?

"For more on pearl-fishing in Sri Lanka, see the work of Tamara Fernando. And Keats's 'Isabella':

> For them the Ceylon diver held his breath,
> And went all naked to the hungry shark;
> For them his ears gush'd blood

Born in 1988, NATALIE SCENTERS-ZAPICO is from El Paso, Texas. She is the author of *Lima :: Limón* (Copper Canyon Press, 2019) and *The Verging Cities* (Center for Literary Publishing, 2015). She won Yale University's Windham Campbell Prize. She teaches at the University of South Florida.

Scenters-Zapico writes: "Much of 'Sentimental Evening' was drafted at a tray table on the back of hospital paperwork after I had an emergency C-section to deliver my son. I then revised it while struggling to breastfeed and submitted it for publication still deep in my postpartum depression. I wrote this poem despite my own internalized misogyny telling me it was too sentimental."

ROBYN SCHIFF was born in New Jersey in 1973. She is the author of four collections of poetry: *Information Desk: An Epic* (Penguin, 2023), *A Woman of Property* (Penguin, 2016), *Revolver* (University of Iowa Press, 2008), and *Worth* (University of Iowa Press, 2002). A coeditor of Canarium Books, she is the recipient of the Joseph Brodsky Rome Prize at the American Academy in Rome. Schiff recently joined the faculty of the University of Chicago.

Schiff writes: "The poem published here is an excerpt from my recent book, *Information Desk: An Epic*, about my experience fielding questions at the information desk at the Metropolitan Museum of Art when I was a young adult. This excerpt begins with the loosing of cockroaches at the Met in an incident of protest in 1969, and continues on to mention a scale insect and a silverfish. These are just a few of the many insects that move variously through *Information Desk*, constituting a subterranean strain of information coursing along with human history."

GJERTRUD SCHNACKENBERG was born in Tacoma, Washington, in 1953. She has published six books of poetry with Farrar, Straus and Giroux.

Of "Strike Into It Unasked," Schnackenberg writes: "Gerard Manley Hopkins's poetry is the most electric, and the most electrifying, poetry I know. Brushing up against his poetry is like touching a live wire without getting hurt. 'The Windhover' exposes a lit-up space, where many different kinds of light are shed all at once, from high-up, out-there, hard-edged sunlight to far-down, far-in, embrous radiance.

"His *The Wreck of the Deutschland* is my favorite poem-of-all-poems, but I don't 'identify with' it, or with Hopkins's, or any other, religious faith. On the contrary, how could I, and why would I, identify with a Victorian Jesuit priest, a poet of still-unfathomed genius, whose tragic life and early death so confound, deprive, and sadden us? But what does agreement have to do with it?

"And how could Hopkins draw a likeness between a raptor and an image of Christ? I wonder if he could have been thinking of the goddesses of the *Iliad* diving at superhuman speeds, 'like hawks,' from Mount Olympus—a world he would not have 'identified with,' but whose cosmic, underlying fire we know he grasped and comprehended in all its stupendous, pagan, raptor-ous, and divine, otherness."

GRACE SCHULMAN, a member of the American Academy of Arts and Letters, received the Poetry Society of America's Frost Medal for distinguished lifetime achievement in American poetry. Her latest of nine books of poems is *Again, the Dawn: New and Selected Poems, 1976–2022* (Turtle Point Press, 2022). She is the author of a memoir, *Strange Paradise: Portrait of a Marriage* (Turtle Point, 2018), and of an essay collection, *First Loves and Other Adventures* (University of Michigan Press, 2010). Editor of *The Poems of Marianne Moore* (Penguin Classics, 2005), she is Distinguished Professor Emerita at Baruch College, CUNY. Schulman directed the Poetry Center at the 92nd Street Y from 1974 to 1984 and was poetry editor of *The Nation* from 1971 until 2006.

Schulman writes: "Inspiration for 'The Night Visitor' goes back to when I stirred to a flamenco dancer in Madrid. Sipping sherry in a café, I was warned to be very quiet while the star dancer, accompanied only by guitar, felt the duende rising within him. In silence, I watched the footwork intricacy call up an urgency I could not identify. Later, I read Lorca's lecture, 'Play and Theory of the Duende,' and realized that artistic inspiration is carried not by a muse that awakens thought, nor by an angel, bathed in light as in Renaissance paintings, but by a demonic spirit that bursts forth in the face of danger and death. It followed that duende was not about death as closure but as the opposite of closure, an opening out to possibility. 'All that has black sounds has duende,' Lorca wrote, and since he gave me the leeway, I discovered those sounds in Rilke's 'every angel terrifies,' in Berryman's 'O powerful despair,' Miles Davis's modals, John Coltrane's mournful sax, and even in Chaïm Soutine's darkly forbidden human subjects. But now I'm torn: my faith is in duende, and yet its expansiveness troubles me. Compelling, yes, but grand, even grandiose. A power I cannot live by. My solution, in 'The Night Visitor,' is to invent my own demon who intrudes at night in place of the cheerier muse. His dark songs, like Lorca's 'black sounds,' draw me to them. In darkness, he lures me to danger—and wild joy."

JANE SHORE was born in Newark in 1947 and grew up over her parents' dress store in North Bergen, New Jersey. She received the 1977 Juniper Prize and the 1986 Lamont Prize. *A Yes-or-No Answer* (Houghton Mifflin Harcourt, 2008) won the 2010 Poet's Prize. A Guggenheim Fellow, a Radcliffe Institute Fellow, and a Hodder Fellow at Princeton, she was awarded two NEA grants. *That Said: New and Selected Poems* was published by Houghton Mifflin Harcourt in 2012. She has taught at Harvard, Tufts, MIT, Sarah Lawrence, the University of Washington, and was the Distinguished Poet-in-Residence at the University of Hawai'i at Manoa. A professor of English at the George Washington University in Washington, D.C., for thirty years, she lives in Vermont. "Who Knows One," the title poem of her new collection, was published in *The Best American Poetry 2019*.

Of "The Hat," Shore writes: "Aunt Roz embodied a time and a place (midcentury New York City) and a world now lost. Artistic but no artist, if only Roz had been lucky enough to have had her own Aunt

Roz to encourage her in the arts, as I did! Arts with a capital A. Roz took me under her wing from the beginning. By becoming a poet and a teacher, I grew up to embody Roz's dream of a life of an artist. (I can't complain.)

"The day that she died, my father phoned me with this dilemma. Roz didn't have a penny, a funeral policy, or a gravesite. Where could we bury her? It would be a shame to dump her in some potter's field, my father said, *among strangers*. We already had our family plot in a New Jersey cemetery, but it was only big enough to fit six bodies, and three spaces were already spoken for—three sudden deaths in the last two years—my grandmother and my mother and my aunt Lil (my father's sister), leaving only my sister's, my father's, and my place left unoccupied. Since I was the older daughter, my father asked me first.

"Would I be willing to give up my spot to Aunt Roz? We couldn't squeeze another body in. So I won't be buried in the family plot. I suppose it's an even exchange. I am who I became in large part because Aunt Roz set me free into the wide world, and Roz occupies the place reserved for me, where I might have been, with the family she was marginalized from, in close proximity, in perpetuity."

MITCH SISSKIND is the author of *Do Not Be a Gentleman When You Say Goodnight* (The Song Cave, 2016) and *Collected Poems 2005–2020*. His poems appeared in *The Best American Poetry* editions for 2009, 2013, and 2023.

Sisskind writes: "For much of the 20th century Jack Benny was one of the best known and most admired comic actors in America. During his career he had his own radio show, his own television sitcom, and he also appeared in films.

"Unlike fast-talking, manic spritzers such as Milton Berle and Jerry Lewis, Benny's comedy was conspicuously restrained and slow paced. Sometimes Jack Benny was funniest when he only stood silently and waited. John Ashbery became a lifelong fan.

"It's wonderful to imagine Ashbery's reaction to a passage in Wikipedia's description of George Burns, Bob Hope, Frank Sinatra, and Ronald Reagan visiting Jack Benny in the hospital—with him (seemingly?) in a coma all the while. It was a perfect Jack Benny ending. He died shortly thereafter, perhaps laughing silently to himself."

MAGGIE SMITH was born in Columbus, Ohio, in 1977. She is the *New York Times* bestselling author of seven books of poetry and prose, including *You Could Make This Place Beautiful* (One Signal/Atria, 2023), *Goldenrod* (One Signal/Atria, 2021), and *Good Bones* (Tupelo Press, 2017). Her most recent book, *My Thoughts Have Wings*, is an illustrated picture book for children (Balzer+Bray/HarperCollins, 2024). She writes, teaches, and edits from her home in Ohio, where she lives with her two children.

Of "Hope Chest," Smith writes: "This poem spun out of the realization that brides are—traditionally, by their fathers—'given away' on their wedding day, and that in my divorce I felt 'given away' again but in a different spirit. What is the opposite of being given away? Taking oneself back."

KAREN SOLIE was born in Moose Jaw in 1966 and grew up in rural southwest Saskatchewan, Canada. Her first collection of poems, *Short Haul Engine* (Brick Books, 2001), won the Dorothy Livesay Poetry Prize. *Pigeon* (Anansi, 2009) won the Pat Lowther Award, the Trillium Poetry Prize, and the Griffin Prize. *The Living Option*, a volume of selected poems, was published in the United Kingdom by Bloodaxe in 2013; a new collection, *Wellwater*, will appear in 2025. She was the 2022 Holloway Visiting Poet at the University of California at Berkeley. She teaches half-time for the University of St. Andrews in Scotland and was awarded a Guggenheim Fellowship in 2023.

Of "The Bluebird," Solie writes: "The perspective of time reveals the wisdom or folly, inconsequence or necessity, of decisions made at crossroads, and the paths branching from those decisions. Once you start thinking about crossroads they proliferate, every choice looks like one, so it's best not to dwell on them. Another aspect of the crossroads is the vantage point. The choice has been made and the path set out upon and at a certain point it becomes clear you can't go back. The vantage point is like a peak above the cloud. There is the uncertain road ahead, the rapidly dissolving reasons lie behind. At the vantage point you reassure yourself that the important thing is to go forward, that it's going to be okay. And sometimes it is, and sometimes it isn't."

Born in Landstuhl, Germany, in 1988, CHRISTOPHER SPAIDE is a poet, critic, and scholar who has taught at Harvard and Emory. The first book of contemporary poetry he remembers buying for himself was *The Best American Poetry 2010*, edited by Amy Gerstler.

Spaide writes: "Three notes on a poem fixated on triads, thirds, and three-peats:

1. 'I'm Not Dying, You're Dying' was written in and about the month of March. Not, canonically speaking, the cruelest month, but in Massachusetts, where I was then living, it's a frontrunner for the crummiest. Far from looking like the glorious season Gerard Manley Hopkins praises in his sonnet 'Spring' (quoted in my epigraph), a Massachusetts March is the triple point of three chaotically coexisting seasons: spring taking its good old time; winter overstaying its welcome; and, once ice thaws and slush sloshes away to reveal grayed, zombified leaves, fall coming back from the dead.

2. That March marked the third anniversary of a death I had commemorated in a scatterbrained elegy titled 'Recycler' (*Poetry*, January 2018). I set out to write a sequel of sorts: an attempt to gauge whether I was moving on, running in circles, or going nowhere.

3. That month—as in most months—I was spending too much time online. Feeling inundated by push notifications, trolly anonymous comments, and headlines summarizing tragedies of every scale (from the next-door to the worldwide), I started toying with the Internet slang crowding out my thoughts: *I'm not crying, you're crying*; Tweets capped with the transparently opaque phrase *asking for a friend*; *rest in peace* abbreviated to a swift, cartoonish monosyllable, *rip*.

"It's been a few springs: what's changed? I still hate March, I keep writing dead-people poems, I couldn't ditch the Internet, but I did leave Massachusetts."

A. (ALICIA) E. STALLINGS was born in 1968. She grew up in Decatur/ Atlanta (where she attended Briarcliff High School, since defunct), attended the University of Georgia in Athens, Georgia, where she studied classics, and now lives in Athens, Greece. Her most recent verse translation, the Pseudo-Homeric *The Battle Between the Frogs and the Mice*, was published by Paul Dry Books in 2019, and *This Afterlife: Selected Poems* came out in 2022 from Farrar, Straus and Giroux. She is currently serving a term as the Oxford Professor of Poetry.

Of "Crown Shyness," Stallings writes: "This is my first sonnet crown, even though the sonnet has been a default mode for me for forever! It isn't that I haven't tried—I've even tried to write a crown about 'crown shyness' between mature trees before (it's one of those facts that fascinates poets), but it was just about trees, and there was not enough 'there' there for more than, say, two complete sonnets. But I've also spent a long time thinking about Homer, and in the last decade particularly about the *Iliad*, and its environmental violence on top of the human destruction. (It's a topical concern: the classicist Edith Hall has a book coming out about the *Iliad* and environmental catastrophe.) I live in Greece, and I often think about how the Aegean islands are denuded of trees, that the landscape we think of as 'Greek' is already the result of deforestation from ancient times, when mature forests were felled to build navies, followed by overgrazing by goats and sheep. Now, of course, the threat is also wildfire. Another thing that obsesses me about the *Iliad* and the *Odyssey* is how, despite being part of the same cycle of stories and with many of the same characters, they are very careful not to overlap at all in terms of narrative. There's an academic term for this, 'Monro's law,' but I have long been thinking about it as a sort of 'crown shyness' of these towering oaks of Western literature. Suddenly I hit upon laying the trees and the epics end to end, and I was finally able to fashion this leafy crown."

MARK STRAND was born to American parents in Summerside, Prince Edward Island, Canada, in 1934, and died in New York City in 2014. He attended Antioch College, the Yale School of Art and Architecture, and the Iowa Writers' Workshop, and became a professor of English at a number of universities, including the University of Utah and Columbia University. He received the Bollingen Prize, the Pulitzer Prize, and a MacArthur Fellowship, and was U.S. Poet Laureate (1990–91). He was also a translator, an essayist, a fiction writer, an author of children's books, and a visual artist and art critic. Strand's work has been translated into many languages. He was guest editor of *The Best American Poetry 1991*.

Mary Jo Salter writes: "The late Mark Strand's appearance in this 2024 anthology is a happy accident, resulting from the discovery last year in the archives at 92NY (formerly known as the 92nd Street Y) a poem by Strand set in that very place. 'Wallace Stevens Comes Back to Read His Poems at the 92nd Street Y' had been accepted in 1994 by *The New Yorker*, which for whatever reason had not published it at the time, and redressed that omission this past year. The poem is *echt* Strand in its voice, both straightforward in diction and musically complex. Note how 'beyond' and 'bound,' words off-rhymed internally, crystallize the theme: 'I loved / The beyond as somebody only can who is bound / By the earth.' And the poem is characteristic too of other poems and prose in which Strand imagined the reappearance of the dead: he tended to treat surrealistic moments with an unsurprised tone of welcome. Strand loved no modern poet more than Wallace Stevens, and wrote about him repeatedly, but the ventriloquizing of the older poet's voice here makes the poem unique. Surely Strand would be pleased by the irony of being revived with Stevens in these pages."

ADRIENNE SU, born in Atlanta, Georgia, in 1967, teaches at Dickinson College in Pennsylvania. She is the author of five books of poetry, most recently *Peach State* (University of Pittsburgh Press, 2021) and *Living Quarters* (Manic D Press, 2015), and one collection of essays, *Hot, Sour, Salty, Sweet* (Paul Dry Books, 2024), which focuses on food and poetry.

Of "The Days," Su writes: "My decision to be a writer happened so early, I can barely remember not having that embodied sense of direction. In youth, I never had trouble answering the question 'What do you want to be when you grow up?' Although the aspiration came with practical difficulties—not least the lack of clear steps to take—one thing always seemed certain: on an everyday basis, writing would be a better choice than not writing.

"That principle has turned out to be sound, in terms of becoming a writer. But the habit of putting words to the page can have unforeseen side effects. Knowing this bothered me enough that I felt compelled to—what else?—write about it."

ARTHUR SZE was born in New York City in 1950. His latest book of poetry is *The Glass Constellation: New and Collected Poems* (Copper Canyon Press, 2021), and he has recently published *The Silk Dragon II: Translations of Chinese Poetry* (Copper Canyon, 2024). His twelfth book of poetry, *Into the Hush*, is forthcoming from Copper Canyon in 2025.

Of "Pe'ahi Light," Sze writes: "My wife, Carol Moldaw, and I were Artists-in-Residence at the Merwin Conservancy in 2022, and I thank Sonnet Kekilia Coggins for that one-month residency at William and Paula Merwin's former home. It was a huge transition for us to move from the high desert landscape of northern New Mexico to a palm forest on Maui. Each morning I got up very early and worked on this sequence of poems at William's former writing desk; I wrote through bird calls and as palm fronds became visible at sunrise. The poem speaks for itself, but I want to add a note about the strike-through lines in section three. I like to use strike-throughs when a speaker reaches a particular point of emotional urgency, and the phrases and their quick, juxtaposed revisions enact the process of a speaker finding greater accuracy of expression. Martin Heidegger once advocated for strike-through lines and wrote, 'Because the words are necessary, they remain legible. Because the words are inaccurate, they are struck through.' "

Born in Minnesota in 1986, CLAIRE WAHMANHOLM is the author of *Wilder* (Milkweed Editions, 2018), *Redmouth* (Tinderbox Editions, 2019), and *Meltwater* (Milkweed Editions, 2023). She was a 2020–2021 McKnight Writing Fellow, and the winner of the 2022 Montreal International Poetry Prize. She lives in the Twin Cities (Minnesota).

Wahmanholm writes: " 'The Field Is Hot and Hotter' is the second sonnet in a crown I wrote during the summer of 2021, currently Minnesota's hottest summer on record (though not for long, I expect). My oldest daughter, around whom the crown revolves, was five. Since she was born, I've been thinking a lot about what survival will look like for her generation: what it will require, how much faster we will need to act in order not to be annihilated, how much we can realistically protect our children from. The sonnet—with its commitments to restriction, interrogation, and love—seemed like the ideal vessel for these questions."

ROSANNA WARREN was born in Connecticut in 1953. She retired from teaching in The Committee on Social Thought at the University of Chicago in June 2023. Her most recent books are a biography, *Max Jacob: A Life in Art and Letters*, and a collection of poems, *So Forth*, both published by W. W. Norton in 2020. She is a member of the American Academy of Arts and Letters, the American Academy of Arts and Sciences, and the American Philosophical Society.

Of "A New Year," Warren writes: "This poem arose from the overnight train ride I often took between Chicago and New York City in the last decade. As usual in my poems, I discover the inner subject by examining an immediate circumstance. In this case, January 2022, hurtling north along the Hudson River led me to muse upon my own aging and our country's aging (and shocking discord), in relation to the ancient geology of the river: more violent—that 'torn uterus of rock' that produced the Hudson—and far older than the woes of our torn and angry country. It's a poem of mourning for a country wretchedly at odds with itself and with its ideals."

Michael Waters's recent books include *Sinnerman* (Etruscan Press, 2023), *Caw* (BOA Editions, 2020) and *The Dean of Discipline* (University of Pittsburgh Press, 2018), as well as a collection of essays, *The Bicycle and the Soul* (Tiger Bark Press, 2024) and a coedited anthology, *Border Lines: Poems of Migration* (Knopf, 2020). A 2017 Guggenheim Fellow, Waters was born in Brooklyn in 1949 and lives without a cell phone in Ocean, New Jersey.

Waters writes: "'Ashkenazi Birthmark' was triggered, in part, by the iconic and haunting photograph known as *The Last Jew in Vinnitsa*, taken during the Holocaust, possibly in April 1942, in Ukraine. Once when I was twenty, I thought that I was dying and, in my terror, saw above me a swirling column, a tornado in which my ancestors hovered, singing, face after face funneling upward into the distant past, and that tornado touched down precisely on the birthmark on my forehead, calming me. My father was Irish Catholic, and I was raised in the Catholic faith, but my mother was Jewish. This poem, written a half-century after that visitation, connects my birthmark to my maternal ancestors."

Eliot Weinberger lives in New York City, where he was born in 1949. His books of literary essays and poetry include *Karmic Traces* (2000), *An Elemental Thing* (2007), *The Ghosts of Birds* (2016), *Angels & Saints* (2020), and *The Life of Tu Fu* (2024), all published by New Directions. His political writings are collected in *What I Heard about Iraq* (Verso, 2005) and *What Happened Here: Bush Chronicles* (New Directions, 2005). The author of a study of Chinese poetry translation, *Nineteen Ways of Looking at Wang Wei* (revised edition, New

Directions, 2016), he translated the poetry of Bei Dao and was the editor of *The New Directions Anthology of Classical Chinese Poetry* (2003). Among his translations of Latin American poetry and prose are *The Poems of Octavio Paz* (New Directions, 2012), Vicente Huidobro's *Altazor* (Wesleyan, 2004), and Jorge Luis Borges's *Selected Non-Fictions* (Penguin, 1999).

Of this excerpt from *The Life of Tu Fu*, Weinberger writes: "This is not a translation of individual poems, but a fictional autobiography derived and adapted from the thoughts, images, and allusions in Tu Fu's poetry."

MATTHEW YEAGER was born in Cincinnati, Ohio, in 1979. *A Big Ball of Foil in a Small NY Apartment*, his micro-budget short film, was an official selection at eleven film festivals in 2009 and 2010, picking up three awards. Since 2011 he has been a cocurator of the KGB Monday Night Poetry Series. Yeager's first book, *Like That*, appeared from Forklift Books in 2016. His second book, *Rocket Surgery*, was published by NYQ books in 2024. His poems have twice appeared in *The Best American Poetry* (2005 and 2010). He is married to the poet Chelsea Whitton and currently teaches at the University of Cincinnati.

Of "The Man with the Yellow Balloon," Yeager writes: "I first attempted to write a poem about a yellow helium balloon dressed up to resemble a 'big idea' comic-strip light bulb in the spring of 2006. Ideally, poems come out quick, smooth, and whole. What causes a poem to take so long? Well, two things: not being able to get it right and an inkling that it's worth getting right.

"The earliest drafts of the 'Yellow Balloon' sounded like a poem of mine from 2005 called 'A Big Ball of Foil in a Small NY Apartment.' The language was bouncy, with a rhythm based in the anapest and the iamb ('It was THEN that he KNEW that the BALL was THERE to STAY'). The poem followed a nameless man as he wore his yellow balloon around the city, and much of its language was used to express the man's thinking. Somehow the poem didn't work.

"In drafting, often a poet will repaint a wall twelve times before he realizes he must knock down the house. Briefly this poem was in couplets. In its 'Man with the Blue Guitar' phase, there was less descriptive language, more playful gratuitous philosophical interjections. The poem was getting worse. There were several drafts called 'The Hat.'

In those, the man was cut out of it. From there, it shrunk down to an E. E. Cummings-ish, goat-footed thing. Unfortunately, there is a digital paper trail. I think I'd totally given up on the poem by 2010.

"At some point in about 2012, Jade Sharma bumped into a draft from 2006. She and her boyfriend at the time, Phil, both thought it was funny. I remember looking at it again and writing a shorter draft (two pages) that looked at the man from a longer view, third person limited, with no access to his thoughts. Then I heard Brenda Shaughnessy read from her book *So Much Synth* in 2016. Her wonderful poem 'But I'm the Only One' made an impression with its amazing recollected chattery social feel, its inclusion of many names of friends, and its pace. I decided to put my own real friends into the yellow balloon poem, to write what their reactions would have been. I wrote most of this version in the spring of 2018 at Yaddo."

KEVIN YOUNG is the author of fifteen books of poetry and prose, including *Stones*; *Blue Laws: Selected & Uncollected Poems 1995–2015*; *Book of Hours*, winner of the Lenore Marshall Prize from the Academy of American Poets; *Jelly Roll: a blues*; *Bunk*; and *The Grey Album*. He is the poetry editor of *The New Yorker*. He is a member of the American Academy of Arts and Sciences, the American Academy of Arts and Letters, and the Society of American Historians. Named a Chancellor of the Academy of American Poets in 2020, he lives and works in Washington, D.C. He was the guest editor of *The Best American Poetry 2011*.

MAGAZINES WHERE THE POEMS WERE FIRST PUBLISHED

---

32 Poems, editor-in-chief George David Clark. www.32poems.com

Able Muse, poetry ed. Stephen Kampa. www.ablemuse.com

The Academy of American Poets Poem-a-Day, guest eds. Diane Seuss (March 2023) and Arthur Sze (December 2022). www.poets.org

AGNI, poetry eds. Jennifer Kwon Dobbs, Jessica Q. Stark, Esteban Rodríguez, Dorsey Craft, Jennie George, Rachel Mennies. www.agnionline.bu.edu

Alaska Quarterly Review, editor-in-chief Ronald Spatz. www.aqreview.org

The American Poetry Review, editor-in-chief Elizabeth Scanlon. www.aprweb.org

The American Scholar, poetry ed. Langdon Hammer. www.theamericanscholar.org

The Atlantic, poetry ed. Walt Hunter. www.theatlantic.com

Bad Lilies, eds. Kathryn Gray and Andrew Neilson. www.badlilies.uk

Bennington Review, ed. Michael Dumanis. www.benningtonreview.org

The Best American Poetry Blog, eds. David Lehman and Stacey Harwood-Lehman. www.blog.bestamericanpoetry.com

The Common, poetry ed. John Hennessy. www.thecommononline.org

Commonweal, senior editor Matthew Boudway. 475 Riverside Drive, Room 244, New York, NY 10115.

Conduit, editor-in-chief William D. Waltz. www.conduit.org

Court Green, eds. Aaron Smith and Tony Trigilio. www.courtgreen.net

Five Points, ed. Megan Sexton. www.fivepoints.gsu.edu

Freeman's, ed. John Freeman. www.freemansbiannual.com

The Gettysburg Review, ed. Mark Drew. www.gettysburgreview.com

Guernica, poetry eds. Sarah Ahmad and Cindy Juyoung Ok. www.guernicamag.com

Guesthouse, poetry ed. Jane Huffman. www.guesthouselit.com

Harper's Magazine, poetry ed. Ben Lerner. www.harpers.org

Harvard Review, poetry ed. Major Jackson. www.harvardreview.org

The Hopkins Review, editor-in-chief Dora Malech. www.hopkinsreview.com

The Hudson Review, ed. Paula Deitz. www.hudsonreview.com

The Kenyon Review, ed. Nicole Terez Dutton. www.kenyonreview.org

Liberties, ed. Leon Wieseltier. www.libertiesjournal.com

Literary Matters, editor-in-chief Ryan Wilson. www.literarymatters.org

Lit Hub, editor-in-chief Jonny Diamond. www.lithub.com

Matter, eds. Virginia Konchan and Glenn Shaheen. www.mattermonthly.com

n+1, eds. Mark Krotov and Dayna Tortorici. www.nplusonemag.com

The New Criterion, poetry ed. Adam Kirsch. www.newcriterion.com

New England Review, poetry ed. Jennifer Chang. www.nereview.com

New Ohio Review, ed. David Wanczyk. www.newohioreview.org

New York Quarterly, poetry eds. Amanda J. Bradly and Délice Williams. www.nyq.org

The New Republic, poetry ed. Rowan Ricardo Phillips. www.newrepublic.com

The New York Review of Books, executive ed. Jana Prikryl. www.nybooks.com

The New Yorker, poetry ed. Kevin Young. www.newyorker.com

Orion, poetry ed. Camille T. Dungy. www.orionmagazine.org

The Paris Review, poetry ed. Srikanth Reddy. www.theparisreview.org

Poetry, ed. Adrian Matejka. www.poetryfoundation.org

Poetry Daily, www.poems.com

Poetry Northwest, ed. Keetje Kuipers. www.poetrynw.org

Prairie Schooner, editor-in-chief Kwame Dawes. www.prairieschooner.unl.edu

Raritan, editor-in-chief Jackson Lears. www.raritanquarterly.rutgers.edu

The Sewanee Review, poetry ed. Eric Smith.
www.thesewaneereview.com

Smartish Pace, ed. Stephen Reichert. www.smartishpace.com

Southern Indiana Review, poetry eds. Rosalie Moffett and El Williams III.
www.usi.edu/sir

The Threepenny Review, ed. Wendy Lesser. www.threepennyreview.com

TriQuarterly, poetry ed. Daniel Fliegel. www.triquarterly.org

Washington Square Review, editor-in-chief Joanna Yas, poetry eds. Clare
Flanagan and Timothy Michalik. www.washingtonsquarereview.com

The Yale Review, ed. Meghan O'Rourke. www.yalereview.org

ACKNOWLEDGMENTS

The series editor wishes to thank Mark Bibbins for his many invaluable contributions. Warm thanks go also to Nin Andrews, Angela Ball, Denise Duhamel, Elaine Equi, Stacey Lehman, Thomas Moody, and Terence Winch; to Glen Hartley and Lynn Chu of Writers' Representatives; and to Kathy Belden, David Stanford Burr, Daniel Cuddy, Madison Thân, Kathryn Kenney-Peterson, and Mia O'Neill at Scribner. The poetry editors of the magazines that were our sources deserve applause; they are the secret heroes of contemporary poetry.

Grateful acknowledgment is made of the magazines in which these poems first appeared and the magazine editors who selected them. A sincere attempt has been made to locate all copyright holders. Unless otherwise noted, copyright to the poems is held by the individual poets.

Kim Addonizio, "Existential Elegy" from *New England Review*. Reprinted by permission of the poet.

Howard Altmann, "Kyiv" from *Commonweal*. Reprinted by permission of the poet.

Julia Alvarez, "Amenorrhea" from *Freeman's*. Reprinted by permission of the poet.

Catherine Barnett, "Apophasis at the All-Night Rite Aid" from *The Game of Boxes*. © 2012 by Catherine Barnett. Reprinted by permission of The Permissions Company, Inc. on behalf of Graywolf Press. Also appeared in *The Kenyon Review*.

Joshua Bennett, "First Philosophy" from *AGNI*. Reprinted by permission of the poet.

April Bernard, " 'Sithens in a net' " from *The World Behind the World*. © 2023 by April Bernard. Reprinted by permission of W. W. Norton. Also appeared in *The New York Review of Books*.

Christopher Childers, "Miasma" from *Smartish Pace*. Reprinted by permission of the poet.

Ama Codjoe, "The Deer" from *The New York Review of Books*. Reprinted by permission of the poet.